Computers
And the Beast of Revelation

Computers and the Beast of Revelation

By David Webber
and Noah Hutchings

HUNTINGTON HOUSE INC.

Copyright © 1986 by David Webber and Noah Hutchings

All rights reserved. No part of this book may be reproduced without permission from the publisher, except by a reviewer who may quote brief passages in a review; nor may any part of this book be reproduced, stored in a retrieval system or copied by mechanical, photocopying, recording or other means, without permission from the publisher.

Huntington House, Inc.
1200 N. Market St., Shreveport, LA 71107

Library of Congress Catalog Card Number 86-80245

ISBN Number 0-910311-37-4

Designed by Don Ellis

Layout and Typesetting by Publications Technologies
Printed in the United States of America

3 4 5 6 7 8 9 0

Table of Contents

Introduction 7
Chapter 1
  The Computers Are Coming! 12
Chapter 2
  Alice In Computerland 24
Chapter 3
  Computer Control 34
Chapter 4
  Computer Networks 47
Chapter 5
  Computer Spies 58
Chapter 6
  Computer Over Beast 70
Chapter 7
  Computer Over People 84
Chapter 8
  An E.F.T. Or An S.D.R. 96
Chapter 9
  Gambling With Credit Cards 105
Chapter 10
  The Ultimate Computer 116
Chapter 11
  The Mark And The Number 127
Chapter 12
  A President For Planet Earth 140
  About The Authors 152

Introduction

The prophet Daniel wrote of the extremity of the age that at *"...the time of the end: many shall run to and fro, and knowledge shall be increased"* (Dan. 12:4). In speaking again of the sequence of end-time events, the prophet said again *"...the end thereof shall be with a flood..."* (Dan. 9:26). The prophetic scope of the world economy at the time of Christ's return depicts a sudden rush of political, financial, and scientific changes that would literally shake the earth to prepare the way for the coming of the "man of sin," the Antichrist. The Word of God indicates quite plainly that the generation of mankind living at the end of the age could witness these dramatic events and know from observing these signs that the coming of the Lord from heaven was at hand, even at the door. *"And when these things begin to come to pass, then look up, and lift up your heads; for your redemption draweth nigh"* (Luke 21:28).

Just as the radio, automobile and airplane appeared almost simultaneously to push mankind into the industrial age, the splitting of the atom, television, and the computer sprang upon the world scene within months of each other to further propel the world into the nuclear and space age.

Primitive computers were used in World War II to convert radar information to firing data for anti-aircraft artillery and naval guns. The first commercial computer did not appear until 1947. But nothing since the creation of Adam has changed the life of man and the world economy in such a brief span as the computer has done. In just 30 years, every facet of modern life has been altered by the computer. If every computer in the world were to suddenly go dead, planes would not fly, trains would not run, traffic lights would not change, banks would have to close, space projects would be aborted, and all department stores and grocery stores would not be able to sell. Today, yes even today, the computer commands the working, buying, and selling of every individual, every business, and every governmental department. If the computers were suddenly silenced, the world would be thrown into instant chaos. Computer numbers and computer code marks are a sign that a checkless and cashless world financial order is coming soon. This will be a precise fulfillment of Revelation 13:16, 17, *"And he causeth all, both small and great, rich and poor, free and bond, to receive a mark in their right hand, or in their foreheads: And that no man might buy or sell, save he that had the mark, or the name of the beast, or the number of his name."*

But no force or entity can produce a power greater than itself. Therefore, inasmuch as by God were all things created, nothing made by the Creator, or His creature — man — can be equal to or greater than the Creator. This is true of the fifth-generation computer, or even a fifty-generation computer. God will always be in control. In these last days when knowledge is increasing, man's inventions mean

INTRODUCTION

divine intervention. To illustrate this point, we refer to a UPI release, dateline Jerusalem, November 26, 1985:

> *Israeli researchers using a computer say they have found encoded messages in the Bible, giving new support to the belief that the Book's every word is divinely inspired. The researchers said in the book of Esther they found a reference to the hanging of ten Nazi war criminals on October 16, 1946, and in the book of Deuteronomy the word "holocaust" was hidden. There is no way to explain this information, said Dr. Moshe Katz, a Technion biomechanic who has a degree in biblical studies. "This is a divine source." The team has drawn no conclusions but if the initial findings hold up, Katz believes the implications could be profound. One of the biggest disputes in the Judeo-Christian tradition has been whether the Bible is literally inspired by God. In Christianity, the question represents a central difference between the theological fundamentalist and the liberal. The team's research suggests the Bible was inspired by God, word for word, letter for letter. Katz said he and Dr. Fred Weiner, a computer specialist on the Technion medical faculty, told the computer to skip letters as it scanned the Hebrew language Bible. Often words, and messages leaped out of the text when the computer used only every 50th letter or 26th letter. One of the Hebrew names for God is Yahweh. When its Hebrew*

letters are translated into numbers, Yahweh becomes number 26. Number 50, Katz points out, is 7 times 7 plus 1. Seven is an important number in the Bible — there are seven days in the week of Creation. It is 50 days between Passover and Shavuot (Pentecost) ... Katz said that by skipping letters the computer found "Elohim," another Hebrew name for God, hidden 147 times among the letters of the book of Genesis. He said the probability of it happening by chance was about one in two million. Computer programmer Dr. Eliyahu Rips, a Hebrew University mathematician, found the name of Aaron the high priest hidden among the letters of the first part of Leviticus 25 times. He said the probability of that happening was one in 500,000. Esther 9 is a story of how Queen Esther demanded the hanging of the ten sons of Haman who were enemies of the Jews. Hidden among the names of the sons were letters of the Hebrew date for 1946 — the year the Nazis were hanged. According to newspaper reports at the time, Julius Streicher, one of the Nazis, shouted just before his hanging, "Today is Purim 1946." Purim is the Jewish holiday celebrating Esther's triumph. The date of the hanging of the Nazis, October 16, 1946, fell on the final day of judgment in the "ten days of awe" between Rosh Hashana and Yom Kippur. In Deuteronomy 31, the Lord told Moses his descendants would forsake God and break his law. Verse 17 says: Then my anger will be kindled against

INTRODUCTION

them ... and I will devour them. When the computer read every 50th letter in that section, the Hebrew word for "holocaust" emerged. Many biblical scholars today believe the Bible was pieced together by a skilled editor using four ancient sources — the "D," "P," "E," and "J" documents. "There is no way that this hypothesis can stand," Katz said, pointing out that many of the encoded words were drawn from passages that proponents of this hypothesis say were pieced together from more than one source. Under the team's theory, if even one letter is removed, all the results collapse.

No word of God in the Bible can be taken away, and no word added. Just as God used the god of the Philistine, Dagan, to prove His power and will, He is today using man's computer-god to prove that though "heaven and earth may pass away, His Word will never pass away." And as we see these signs passing rapidly before our eyes, we pray with the apostle John, "Even so, come, Lord Jesus."

Noah Hutchings

1
THE COMPUTERS ARE COMING!

We are living in an age of knowledge explosion.

This vast increase in knowledge was prophesied by the prophet Daniel.

Our Lord — in His discourse on Mt. Olivet and by His word to John in the revelation — also warned of the time when man's knowledge would increase without a corresponding increase in man's moral capability to handle it. Thus it would lead to a time of unprecedented lawlessness and mass destruction.

Remember that Satan promised Eve that knowledge in itself leads to God-likeness.

It is our desire to awaken you to the fact of this great age of information, this explosion of knowledge. To accomplish that task, we want to share with you information about computer control, computer networks, computer spies, the ultimate computer and other subjects — all in light of Bible prophecy.

The inability of man to control knowledge without God is reflected in an editorial by Fred J. Deering that appeared in the December 30, 1974 edition of *The Daily Oklahoman:*

> ... *Opinion surveys show that people are losing confidence in the institutions of society — governmental, religious, educational, familial and commercial. Immorality is destroying our morale ... Today's outlaw children have not been taught the difference between right and wrong, or why they should do right. Great numbers of them have never heard of the Ten Commandments ... Schools were created to serve as extensions of the home to expand the youngster's knowledge of academic fundamentals, ways of life and ways of earning a living. It may be somewhat more than a coincidence that the current deterioration of the home was accelerated about the time the schools abandoned McGuffey's Readers and other textbooks that emphasized traditional American values. Schools now may use textbooks that are anti-American, anti-business and anti-civilization. Teachers may instruct pupils in the theory of evolution but not in the story of creation. They may teach or demonstrate immorality but religious instruction is subject to protest under negative rulings of the Supreme Court ... textbooks ... contain writings and material so obscene that this newspaper cannot publish the worst examples. But they may be read by pupils ....*

Knowledge without God always leads to destruction. We read in Romans 1:22-24, "Professing themselves to be wise, they became fools ... wherefore God also gave them up ..." The summation of what is troubling our world today is found later in the same chapter, verse 28, "And even as they did not like to retain God in their knowledge, God gave them over to a reprobate mind ...."

There is nothing wrong with knowledge and education when they are used for the good of man and to the glory of God. Daniel, one of the greatest of the prophets, was a young scientist when he was taken captive to Babylon. There is nothing wrong with schools, or any kind of educational, scientific, or mathematical aids like computers, when they are used to promote good will, peace, and freedom on earth. So the evil is not in knowledge or machines, but rather in the sin that lies within the human heart. And today, this vast knowledge that is available to man is being used to magnify his rebellion against God.

We read the headline from an article on computer science that appeared on page 50 of the June 30, 1980 edition of *Newsweek,* "And Man Created the Chip."

Thus, God created man, and man then created the chip. The inference here is that when man created the computer chip, he didn't need God anymore. This satanic propaganda, though not stated explicitly, is implied in articles like the one previously referred to in *Newsweek:*

> *"Welcome! Always glad to show someone from the early '80s around the place. The biggest change, of course, is the*

THE COMPUTERS ARE COMING

smart machines — they're all around us. No need to be alarmed, they're very friendly. Can't imagine how you lived without them. The telephone, dear old thing, is giving a steady busy signal to a bill collector I'm avoiding ... The oven already knows the menu for tonight, and the kitchen robot will mix us a mean martini. Guess we're ready. Oh no, you won't need a key. We'll just program the lock to recognize your voice and let you in whenever you want.

"A revolution is under way ... We are at the dawn of the era of the smart machine ... an 'Information Age' that will change forever the way an entire nation works, plays, travels and even thinks. Just as the Industrial Revolution dramatically expanded the strength of man's muscles and the reach of his hand, so the smart-machine revolution will magnify the power of his brain. But unlike the Industrial Revolution, which depended on finite resources such as iron and oil, the new Information Age will be fired by a seemingly endless resource — the inexhaustible supply of knowledge itself. Even computer scientists, who best understand the galloping technology and its potential, are wonderstruck by its implication. 'It is really awesome,' says L.C. Thomas of Bell Laboratories. 'Every day is just as scary as the day before.'

"The driving force behind the revolution is the development of two fundamental and interactive technologies — computers and integrated circuits. Today, tiny silicon chips

16   COMPUTERS AND THE BEAST

half the size of a fingernail are etched with circuitry powerful enough to book seats on jumbo jets, keep the planes working smoothly in the air, help children learn to spell and play chess well enough to beat all but the grandest masters. The new technology means that bits of computing power can be distributed wherever they might be useful ... this 'computational plenty' is making smart machines easier to use and more forgiving of unskilled programming. Machines are even communicating with each other. 'What's next?' asks Peter E. Hart, director of the SRI International artificial-intelligence center. 'More to the point, what's not next?' "

On the front cover of the June 30, 1980 edition of *Newsweek* magazine is a computer screen unit with the computer readout, "Hello, I am your friend Chip. I'm getting smarter all the time. Soon I will be everywhere. And by my instant calculations society will never be the same."

Also visible on the cover is the usual computer code mark that now appears on all items that are bought and sold. As the article brings out, nothing is now impossible in the computer field. As stated in Genesis 1:27, God created man in His own image, and God said in Genesis 11:6 that what man can imagine, that he can do. So knowledge, imagination and material govern the computerized society of tomorrow. Knowledge has increased over a thousandfold in our generation, man's imagination is now without limitations, and the material is no problem because the computer chip is made out of

THE COMPUTERS ARE COMING 17

silicon, or common sand. What happens next? The Bible states plainly in Revelation 13:16-18 that in the last days no one will buy, sell or work except by the means of a mark, or code mark, in their hand or on their forehead.

Some computer experts, perhaps to calm the fears that computer machines may take over the earth, have denied that computer-controlled robots can actually think and reason for themselves. But take note of the following news release that appeared in the October 10, 1974 edition of *The Daily Oklahoman* ... "NASA experimenting with thinking robots":

> *"A robot that can think for itself is being studied by the National Aeronautics and Space Administration for possible use in exploring the surface of outer planets of the solar system. The problem with the type of robot such as the Soviets used to explore the moon is the time it takes for radio signals to travel from the earth to a planet such as Mars. The Soviet unit used on the moon was totally controlled by a human operator driving and directing it by remote control from the earth. The time required for radio signals to make the round trip to the moon is about three seconds, so the time lag between ... was not too great. On Mars, however, the delay would be at least six minutes and at parts of the orbit of Mars the delay could reach 15 minutes. This means that the robot traveling on the surface of Mars could 'see' with its television cameras the approach of a steep cliff, but between*

> *the time the cliff first came into view and when the operator on earth received the view there would be at least one 6-minute delay ... The eventual goal is a robot vehicle which can go about its business of studying the surface of a planet ..."*

Scientists are in the process of making a computerized robot that will look much like a man, have the mobility of a man and not only think like a man, but solve problems in seconds that require years for a man to answer. One reason for these thinking robots is to explore other planets, but the obvious conclusion is also presented — the using of these robots for all kinds of jobs that are difficult or unpleasant for men.

The book of Joel deals with many problems of mankind near the end of the age, and particularly during the last few years. And if you do not think that the human race has problems today, then you have not been reading your daily newspaper or listening to the 6:00 news. Consider this portion of Joel's prophecy that relates to a time just preceding the return of Jesus Christ, and see if you do not relate this dark prophecy to an invading computerized, robot army, armed with nuclear weapons:

> *"Blow ye the trumpet in Zion, and sound an alarm in my holy mountain: let all the inhabitants of the land tremble: for the day of the Lord cometh, for it is nigh at hand; A day of darkness and of gloominess, a day of clouds and of thick darkness, as the morning spread upon the mountains: a great people and a strong; there hath not been ever the*

like, neither shall be any more after it, even to the years of many generations. A fire devoureth before them; and behind them a flame burneth: the land is as the garden of Eden before them, and behind them a desolate wilderness; yea, and nothing shall escape them. The appearance of them is as the appearance of horses; and as horsemen, so shall they run. Like the noise of chariots on the tops of mountains shall they leap, like the noise of a flame of fire that devoureth the stubble, as a strong people set in battle array. Before their face the people shall be much pained: all faces shall gather blackness. They shall run like mighty men; they shall climb the wall like men of war; and they shall march every one on his ways, and they shall not break their ranks: Neither shall one thrust another; they shall walk every one in his path: and when they fall upon the sword, they shall not be wounded. They shall run to and fro in the city; they shall run upon the wall, they shall climb up upon the houses; they shall enter in at the windows like a thief. The earth shall quake before them; the heavens shall tremble: the sun and the moon shall be dark, and the stars shall withdraw their shining" (Joel 2:1-10).

Joel prophesied that this strange army, like men, will climb walls, detour around obstacles, and march in rank. They will go through fire and not be burned, they will run forward without jostling against one another, and be hit by objects hurled or fired in battle, yet their advance will not be halted. Joel seemed certain about what God showed him in this vision of war at the time the Lord comes, but I do not believe the world has yet witnessed an army in battle like the prophet saw. However, with the use of thinking robots that can climb walls and go around obstacles to carry out their mission, we are indeed near that time when such an army of computerized soldiers may be employed in conflict.

Dr. Robert Jastrow, director of NASA's Goddard Institute for Space Studies, stated in an article titled "Toward An Intelligence Beyond Man's" appearing in the February 20, 1978, edition of *Time* magazine:

> "As Dr. Johnson said in a different era about ladies preaching, the surprising thing about computers is not that they think less well than a man, but that they think at all. The early electronic computer did not have much going for it except a prodigious memory and some good math skills, but today the best models can be wired up to learn by experience, follow an argument, ask pertinent questions and write pleasing poetry and music.
>
> "They can also carry on somewhat distracted conversations so convincingly that their human partners do not know they are talking to a machine
>
> "... As computers get more complex, the imitation gets better. Finally, the line between the original and the copy becomes blurred. In another 15 years or so ... we will see the computer as an emergent form of life. The proposition seems ridiculous

because, for one thing, computers lack the drives and emotions of living creatures. But when drives are useful, they can be programmed into the computer's brain, just as nature programmed them into our ancestor's brain as a part of the equipment for survival. For example, computers, like people, work better and learn faster when they are motivated. Arthur Samuel made this discovery when he taught two IBM computers how to play checkers. They polished their game by playing each other, but they learned slowly..

"Finally, Dr. Samuel programmed in the will to win by forcing the computers to try harder — when they were losing. Then the computers learned very quickly. One of them beat Samuel and went on to defeat a champion player who had not lost a game to a human opponent in eight years. Computers match people in some roles, and when fast decisions are required in a crisis, they often outclass them ....

"We are still in control, but the capabilities of computers are increasing at a fantastic rate, while raw human intelligence is changing slowly, if at all.

"Computer power is growing exponentially; it has increased evolution — vacuum tubes, transistors, simple integrated circuits and today's miracle chips — followed one another in rapid succession, and the fifth generation, built out of such esoteric devices as bubble memories and

> *Josephenson junctions, will be on the market in the 1980s."*

The article continues to relate that a man and computer in the future can so work together that something will be produced that will be beyond human intelligence. Once more it is evident that Satan is still attempting to make good his promise to Eve that she and Adam would become as gods if they would eat of the tree of knowledge. Recently on national television a movie was shown where computers rebelled against their human partners, killed the leaders, and put computer-like replicas in their places. Then the human race became slaves of the computers. According to Dr. Jastrow's article, such a fantasy could at some future time become reality.

Here's a description of the ultimate computer from a secular publication, *National Enquirer*, December 13, 1983: "A Super Computer Will Solve All Our Problems — And Even Crack Jokes."

> *"The ultimate computer will look like a giant robot and act like a human being — making lightning-fast decisions on its own, feeling human emotions like friendship, and even cracking jokes.*
>
> *"There will be one super-brain for the whole world. Housed in a 10-foot-high body, it will search out and solve mankind's problems — crime, ill health, bad weather, traffic jams, etc.*
>
> *"That's how futurists like Saul Kent — author of* The Life-Extension Revolution *— visualize the ultimate computer of tomorrow.*

> 'The ultimate computer will not only be endowed with many human characteristics, designers will construct it in a human like form so they can treat it as much like a human as possible,' said Kent. 'It could be a colossal robot up to 10 feet high — and it will be mobile, able to move itself in case of a war. And it will develop traits characteristic of a human personality.' "

You can readily see that this giant lifelike robot would be very impressive, and, of course, in the beginning it would be helping people, so this electronic superhero would be the good guy in this end-time scenario. But a colossus with these electronic capabilities could easily become the Big Brother of the beast system watching you (see Rev. 13).

All the computers in the world and all the knowledge in the world cannot purify the heart of man to qualify him to control the lives of others. Only Jesus Christ can cleanse a man from sin and make him a new creature.

2
Alice in Computerland

Mankind has stumbled into the amazing modern world much like Alice stumbled into her Wonderland. The world of today is just as different from the world of one hundred years ago as Alice's dream world was from the world of reality. During the lifetime of a 40-year-old person alive today, the following events have changed the social and political complexion of planet Earth:

The atom has been split and nuclear devices made that can destroy the entire human race.

The final breakup of the old Roman Empire, and the colonial powers of Europe.

The forming of a Revived Roman Empire from the uniting of the 10 nations.

The development of a space exploration program that has sent men to the moon and spaceships to Mars, Jupiter, Venus, and beyond.

The divorce rate has increased from one in eight marriages to one in two marriages. The crime rate has increased by approximately 500 percent.

Israel has been restored as a nation, and the Middle East once more has become the focus of the economic and political attention of all nations.

Instant radio and television communications, enabling news at any one spot to be broadcast or telecast to every nation in a matter of seconds. The invention and development of computers that will soon abolish all money and dictate to every man, woman, and child that they must work, buy, and sell by using code marks and numbers.

In spite of all the scientific wizardry and political developments of our age, the world masses for the most part seem hypnotized with the wonder of it all. If we could go back one hundred years in time and look upon mankind in the setting of 1980, it would appear that the average person today is like a man caught in a nightmare, hoping that he wakes before he plunges over a precipice into oblivion.

Yet, over twenty-five hundred years ago, the Creator who lives in eternity, and does not have to wait for the unfolding of time to forecast the future, instructed a man by the name of Daniel to write, "But thou, O Daniel, shut up the words, and seal the book, even to the time of the end: many shall run to and fro, and knowledge shall be increased" (Dan. 12:4).

Concerning the fulfillment of the prophecy from Daniel, we refer to a quotation from *The Beginning of the End* by Tim LaHaye (pg. 90):

> "Today we have cars that travel at 600 (mph), planes that hurtle through the air at 2,000 mph, and spaceships at 24,000 miles per hour ... A quick look at history will show that back in 1913, when Henry Ford organized the first assembly line and mass

produced one million Model T Fords, the riding speed was about 25 miles per hour. The next year the world was thrust into World War I, the great sign of the end, and this catapulted all nations into a race to transport men 'to and fro' ... About ten years ago the telephone company put out a booklet about the speed of travel ... it contained a graph showing the rate at which speeds have increased. The line of speed paralleled the line of history for centuries. About the middle of the nineteenth century, it started up slightly; after World War I it made a sharp incline; and today the chart line is going almost straight up. The telephone company did not realize it was graphically illustrating the fulfillment of Bible prophecy."

From a speed of 30 miles an hour, one of the restraining bonds of God, in just 60 years man was propelled to speeds in excess of 600 miles per hour on the ground, 2,000 mph in the air, and 20,000 mph in outer space. But such a rapid and sudden acceleration of travel is prophesied in the Bible for the end of the age. It is evident from Zechariah 14:1,2; Rev. 16:12-16; Rev. 19:11-21; and many other prophetic Scriptures, that armies of every nation will be gathered together in the Middle East within the span of a few days. Such a sudden marshalling of the armed forces of all nations was not possible before this present generation.

During the same period when the speed at which man could travel was being moved forward from 30 mph to 20,000 mph, there has been a corresponding advancement in methods of

ALICE IN COMPUTERLAND

communication. Before the 20th century, weeks, and possibly months, were required for a letter posted in Jerusalem to reach Washington D.C. Today, the prime minister of Israel is not more than a few seconds away from the president of the United States by telephone, radio, or television. The apostle Paul, by inspiration of God, prophesied in 2 Thessalonians 2:4 that before Jesus Christ returned to planet Earth to bring an end to the dispensation of grace in which we now live, an ungodly world dictator would sit in the temple in Jerusalem proclaiming himself as God to all the people of the world. Such a thing was not possible before the invention of television.

We read also of two men endowed with power from God who will be killed by this world dictator in Jerusalem: "And they of the people and kindreds and tongues and nations shall see their dead bodies three days and a half, and shall not suffer their dead bodies to be put in graves" (Rev. 11:9). Pictures of the dead witnesses of God will be shown to all nations for three and one-half days. Again, such an event would not have been possible before the launching of Telstar, bringing international television communications.

Correspondingly, at the time of the end when travel and communications expand upward, the prophet Daniel said there would be an increase of knowledge. Experts disagree among themselves as to just how fast man's knowledge is increasing, but all agree that we are in the midst of an unprecedented educational explosion. Some say that the combined knowledge of man is doubling every 10 years, some say that it is doubling every five years, and still others contend it is doubling every two and one-half years. But even the 10-year figure is startling beyond belief.

The illustration has been made to allow one inch on a yardstick to represent all of the accumulation of the knowledge of man from Adam to the year 1940 A.D. In 1940 the knowledge line began to rise sharply, and today, it has not only increased 36 times and plunged off the top of the yardstick, but it has climbed all the way to the top of the Washington Monument, a distance of 555 1/2 feet.

To again impress us with the "Alice in Wonderland" aspects of our modern world as viewed from one hundred years ago, we refer once more to the book, *The Beginning of the End* (pg. 94):

> *"It has been estimated that 70 percent of the medicines in use today were developed after World War II. More than 90 percent of the scientists who have ever lived are alive today! And high-speed computers can classify and sort information today in unbelievable time ... The quest for knowledge goes on at an ever-heightening pace. College enrollments are exploding all over the world. In our own country, the number of college students has doubled in the last decade. Today 46 percent of America's youth between the ages of eighteen and twenty-one are attending some kind of post-high school institution. We hear a great deal about revolution today, little noticing that a revolution in knowledge is going on all around us. Have you looked at your children's textbooks lately?... A group of psychiatrists in Los Angeles a few*

months ago had a conference to consider the knowledge explosion and its effect on the family. Their solution was typically humanistic. Due to the fact that parents were not keeping up with the increase of knowledge, and in order to keep from retarding the rate of their children's learning, the government should make plans to raise our children in the future they said! During the last twenty years the computer has revolutionized many forms of research and learning ... The Sperry Rand Corporation has developed a memory bank which can assimilate the 850,000 words in the Bible five times in one second!"

The ability of the human mind to learn, assimilate, and project, reached its limit in 1940, and this is where the computer came into the end-time picture. To illustrate the role the computer is playing in the knowledge explosion, note the July, 1974 edition of *The Midnight Cry:*

"Without the computer, our astronauts would never have been able to perform their space missions. For example, in April of 1970, the U.S. Apollo XIII mission was suddenly aborted and the decision made to bring the crippled ship back to earth. It took scientists working with computers only 84 minutes to figure the correct return path to earth. How long do you suppose it would have taken a mathematical brain to do this? Well, NASA figures it would have taken one

> *man using just pencil and paper more than a million years to perform the task."*

Let us suppose that Adam was created with brain power equal to that of a scientist today holding a doctor's degree, and we believe that he was. Let us also suppose that God gave Adam a problem to work concerning the relativity of time, space, and matter. On January 1, 1979, Adam rushes into our space center waving a paper with the answer he has just arrived at after almost 6,000 years. A girl at a computer takes the same problem to check the answer, and in just 30 seconds, she turns to Adam and verifies his answer. This is how fast the modern computer has speeded up scientific knowledge: 6,000 years compared to 30 seconds.

Soon, computers will be installed in every classroom in America, beginning at the grade-school level. An article in the *U.S. News & World Report* of January 2, 1978 (dateline Flint, Michigan), states in part:

> *"Students in the city's schools learn their lessons in a setting that looks more like a space control center than a classroom. The young scholars are using computer terminals to help them do much of their work ... At Northern Community High School, the advanced physics class learns the principles of motion and Newton's Second Law of gravity by making simulated lunar landings. The terminals print out the amount of fuel, speed, and the rate of descent, and students make split-second calculations to avoid a crash ...."*

ALICE IN COMPUTERLAND

The June 1980 edition of *OMNI* magazine, in an article titled "Electronic Tutors," made the following observation:

> *"We are now witnessing one of the swiftest and most momentous revolutions in the entire history of technology ... just a decade ago, the invention of the pocket calculator made the slide rule obsolete almost overnight, and with it whole libraries of logarithmic and trigonometric tables. There has never been so stupendous an advance in so short a time ... Pocket calculators are already having a profound effect on the teaching of mathematics, even at the level of elementary arithmetic. but they are about to be succeeded by devices of much greater power and sophistication — machines that may change the very nature of the educational system ... Where does this leave the human teacher? Well, let me quote this dictum: any teacher who can be replaced by a machine should be!"*

The world of tomorrow has arrived when machines can talk. As the ultimate example consider the article about Cray 2, *Time* Magazine, June 17, 1985, entitled "A Sleek Superpowered Machine":

> *"With its black frame, red Naugahyde base and transparent plastic panels, it looks like a cross between a recreation room bar and an aquarium. Its blue-tinted towers, washed by 200 gallons of liquid coolant,*

bubble and shimmer like overheated Lava Lites. Its nickname is 'Bubbles', and it bears little resemblance to the computers that most Americans have seen. But the $17.6 million Cray-2 is a computer — a supercomputer at that — and it is the fastest one in operation today. Last week in a brightly-lit room at Lawrence Livermore National Laboratory in Livermore, Calif., the first production model of the Cray-2 gurgled and glowed, and a nearby printer spewed out a string of characters: $905. B D/U WO/F 06/04 15:24:22 16a. Software Manager Dieter Fuss stared at the message and interpreted it for the assembled Livermore technicians and executives: 'It just came alive and said: I'm ready.' In that moment, a new era of high-speed computing began. The Cray-2 has the world's largest internal memory capacity (2 billion bytes) and a top speed of 1.2 billion FLOPS (floating point, or arithmetical operations per second), six to twelve times faster than its predecessor, the Cray-1, and 40,000 to 50,000 times faster than a personal computer. It outdistances the world's half-dozen other super-computers-machines specially designed to carry out vast numbers of repetitive calculations at incredible speeds — and is expected to make short work of problems that have vexed scientists and engineers for decades. Says Robert Borchers, Lawrence Livermore's associate director for computations: 'What took a year in 1952 we can now do in a second.' Who needs such

› *blinding speed? ... U.S. intelligence agencies depend on supercomputers to sort through the enormous quantities of surveillance data beamed home by ground-based listening posts and orbiting spy satellites. By using supercomputers to simulate explosion, nuclear weapons experts require fewer test explosions to validate their designs. Machines like the Cray-2 are essential to any Star Wars defensive system for locating and intercepting incoming missiles before they re-enter the atmosphere."*

For centuries, Bible scholars have wondered how Revelation 13 could ever be fulfilled, when some kind of an image, or a machine, could speak and command everyone in the world to work, buy, and sell with code marks and numbers. A few decades ago it was easier for people to believe in Alice's talking rabbit or Queen of Hearts than a talking machine. The world today is even more amazing than the Wonderland of Alice, but where is it all leading? The Bible indicates these are signs of the coming Antichrist, but Jesus said in Matthew 24:44, "Therefore be ye also ready: for in such an hour as ye think not, the Son of man cometh." The lesson our Lord was teaching was that in the end of the age, if we know Him as our Lord and Savior, we can be ready for anything.

3
COMPUTER CONTROL

The item that dominates the world's news media today is rampaging computer technology. Computer scientists contend that within 10 years the computer will control mankind's total being. This awesome power that is destined to guide the destiny of the human race is causing many experts to wonder if man is not now in the process of creating his own god. Amazingly, it is not primarily the leaders and spokesmen for religion that are expressing concern, but rather the computer makers themselves. Some are attempting to justify the neo-godly aspects of the new computers by explaining that it really does not make any difference, because God is in the computer.

On page 40 of the May, 1984 edition of *Science* appears a lengthy article titled "Computer Worship." This article begins with a full-page color picture of a computer on the altar in a church with a beam of light from heaven illuminating its presence for the worship service. The authors present the claim by computer experts that in the future, students will not need to master reading, writing or arithmetic. All that will be

COMPUTER CONTROL

needed to equip young people to meet life's challenges is to learn how to operate the new generation of computers.

To emphasize the danger of a controlled computerized world order, we refer to the April 10, 1978, edition of *U.S. News & World Report:*

> *"Aroused by increasing fears of government snooping, Americans are taking a hard look at the spread of electronic computers throughout the federal bureaucracy ... At the heart of the controversy is the explosive growth in the government's use of data-processing equipment. Scattered throughout the bureaucracy are 11,000 computers of all sizes and types — twice as many as there were five years ago. It takes some 150,000 people to operate and maintain these machines, at a cost of about 10 billion dollars a year ... More recently, however, powerful electronic machines have been developed and put into use. They are capable of making judgments and decisions that heretofore were reserved for managers ... Authorities agree that, as highly efficient processors of information, computers are extremely useful to society. 'Without computers it would be impossible for the government to function,' asserts Walter Haase, deputy associate director for information-systems policy in the Office of Management and Budget ... with some 3.9 billion records on persons stored in thousands of federal data systems, there is mounting concern that the computers could be manipulated with equal efficiency to*

> control, intimidate or harass the citizenry. Available in government computers is a vast array of data on virtually every American, including personal finances ... David F. Linowes, who headed the Privacy Protection Study Commission, asks: 'What happens if this data that's being collected gets into the wrong hands?' There is no reason to believe that someone won't come along at some point to abuse it ... In fact, there already have been several attempts by the bureaucracy to create powerful computer networks, all in the name of improved efficiency. One of the most ambitious plans to surface so far was a project of the General Services Administration known as FEDNET."

Many in our country who are in charge of law and order, even though they might abhor the Communist suppression of human rights, nevertheless admire the efficiency of their people control system. The September 28, 1970 edition of *The National Bulletin* carried the following report:

> "The invention of the telephone was greeted as being the miracle of electronics — an instantaneous method of personal and private communications.
>
> The only people who had anything to fear from using the instrument were criminals and people dealing in subversive activities ... But the way things are going now, every subscriber to the telephone will find himself completely robbed of all privacy. Plans are underway to have every

> telephone installation automatically bugged by computers linked directly with ... central memory banks ...
>
> One knowledgeable person is David Hutchinson of Brooklyn, New York, (who said), 'We were making bugging devices for regular court-order type tapping operations carried out by the police authorities and so on. But then we received a fantastic order from AT&T for the miniature monitoring systems that fit right inside the receiver. I later found out that the telephone companies are working hand in hand with the FBI, CIA and everyone else, to form a complete dossier of personal information on every citizen throughout the United States' ...."

This article continues to claim that mass experimental bugging programs were instituted in the Dallas and Los Angeles areas.

A vision of the perfect computerized man of the Fifth Generation is described in an article titled, "What next? A World of Communications Wonders," page 59 of the April 9, 1984 edition of *U.S. News & World Report*:

> "A phone in every pocket, a computer in every home: That and more await consumers as astonishing information age techniques start to pay off. A global telecommunications revolution is poised to bring astonishing changes to virtually every American — especially anyone who picks

up a telephone, switches on a television set or logs on to a computer. Growing out of the marriage of communications links with modern computers, the new technologies are spreading lightning fast. Experts say that the upheaval won't end until anyone, anywhere can reach out and touch anyone else — instantly and effortlessly — through electronics. Among the extraordinary possibilities in store for consumers by the end of this century:

"•The standard telephone console will become the only computer terminal most people will need. Text and pictures will be viewed on a video screen attached to the phone, and additional data will be delivered as electronically synthesized speech. Phone users also will be able to see who is calling before answering.

"•Combining laser optics and computers, three-dimensional holographic images will bring TV features into living rooms with almost lifelike clarity.

"•Automobiles will have not only telephones as standard equipment but also satellite navigation devices to pinpoint a vehicle's location and guide the driver to any destination.

"•Automatic-translation devices will allow people to insert a text in English and have it delivered in minutes to a distant point in Japanese, Arabic or one of many other languages.

"Already, the conduits of yesterday — copper wires, radio signals, ground

COMPUTER CONTROL 39

antennas and even electricity itself — are giving way to glass fibers, microwaves, satellites, laser beams and the pulsating digital languages of computers. The economic potential of such unprecedented changes in communications technology is practically limitless: Sales of hardware alone reached $60 billion in 1983 ... Like a summer vine that shoots out in every direction without discernible pattern, the telecommunications grip also is spreading uncontrollably. Never before have so many individuals and organizations been able to interact on such a vast scale. By the end of the century, electronic information technology will have transformed American business, manu-facturing, school, family, political and home life ... says William McGowan, chairman of MCI Communications Corporation: 'Telecommunications is one business today in which you don't need losers to have winners. There is enough for everybody. The instruments in this sweeping electronic upheaval — computers, electronic links and video technologies — are the interlocking parts of a communications network undreamed of only a decade ago.'"

A bulletin from *The Research Institute of America* dated April 1984 states:

"Computers are playing an oven larger role as diagnostic tools ... Computers are invading doctor's offices in growing numbers. Cooperation between medical

doctors and computer scientists has become a rapidly growing area of specialization."

The article continues to attest that in diagnosing diseases in 500 individuals, the computers were better than doctors. The authors of *The Fifth Generation* go into more detail about the potentials and qualifications of "Dr. Computer." Note page 87:

> "Many kinds of expertise are unevenly distributed in the world. Medicine is a perfect example. That is one reason the U.S. National Institutes of Health have been at the forefront of supporting expert systems research ... If the idea of a machine doctor repels you, consider that not everyone feels that way. Studies in England showed that many humans were much more comfortable with an examination by a computer terminal than with a human physician, whom they perceived as somehow disapproving of them. 'Mechanical' doctors are inferences and drawing conclusions. They often outperform the very experts who have programmed them because of their methodical ways; they don't skip or forget things, get tired or rushed, or fall subject to some of our other human failings. They will be on call at the patient's convenience, not just the physician's. And they can bring medicine to places where none now exists."

The Fifth Generation computer has been on the drawing boards since 1978. The American computer industry, which has led the world in computer

COMPUTER CONTROL 41

technology, has been reticent to bring in the Fifth Generation Age because it has been uncertain what it would do to human society in economics, education, military defense, science, politics and religion. However, Japan has now forced computer scientists in the United States into a decision. They must now produce these new machines, which some contend will not be machines at all, but organic, thinking entities. If the United States' computer industry fails to produce the Fifth Generation computer, then Japan will conquer the world market. This amounts to a computer Pearl Harbor.

We quote from page 12 of *The Fifth Generation:*

"The Japanese are planning the miracle product. It will come not from their mines, their wells, their fields, or even their seas. It comes instead from their brains. The miracle product is knowledge, and the Japanese are planning to package and sell it the way other nations package and sell energy, food, or manufactured goods. They're going to give the world the next generation — Fifth Generation — of computers, and those machines are going to be intelligent ... In October 1981, when Japan first let the world at large know about its plans for the Fifth Generation of computers, the Japanese government announced that over the next decade it planned to spend seed money of $450 million and would eventually involve several hundrod top scientists in this project. Their goal is to develop computers for the 1990s and beyond — intelligent computers that will be able to converse with humans in

> *natural language and understand speech and pictures. These will be computers that can learn, associate, make inference, make decisions, and otherwise behave in ways we have always considered the exclusive province of human reason."*

The authors of *The Fifth Generation* continue to quote Japanese sources which claim that the new biocomputers will solve the world's unemployment, energy shortages, medical costs, problems that come with old age, industrial inefficiency, food shortages and money crises. It has been estimated by one computer expert that all the memory and data that is in all the present computers in all the world could be stored in a space no bigger than a sugar cube in a Fifth Generation computer.

Governments in all nations are one of the biggest users of computers, and computers are rapidly taking over jobs once performed by bureaucrats. An article on page 61 of the April 2, 1984 *U.S. News and World Report* states in part:

> *"Wherever he goes, Treasury Secretary Donald Regan takes along a portable computer that he uses to keep abreast of a wide range of fast-changing economic data fed from Washington ... At least two Supreme Court Justices now write their formal court opinions on electronic word processors ... In 1983, the government spent some 12 billion dollars — double the amount of five years earlier — to purchase, operate and maintain 18,000 large and medium-sized computers. Not included are*

COMPUTER CONTROL

> *hundreds of thousands of small computers ... Under a five-year plan begun last April, the government's computer expenditures will total 28 billion dollars by 1988 ... Recently the Internal Revenue Service got a green light to proceed with a sweeping modernization program that could have a profound effect on American attitudes about paying taxes. This year the IRS began using optical-character recognition equipment to process some 18 million tax returns ...*
>
> *"The scanners, which can read, number and perform all other processing of the forms at the rate of 10,000 operations per hour, will allow close examination of far more returns than ever before ... Computer matching is rapidly becoming a routine way to ferret out waste and abuse throughout the government ... Computer specialists say that changes in the way the government delivers services are just beginning. They predict savings of billions of dollars as more sophisticated computers take over routine bureaucratic assignments."*

On an international basis the computer is merging all nations into a single economic system. We quote from an article titled "Telecommunications: The Global Battle" on page 126 of the October 24, 1983 *Business Week:*

> *"That world (the world of yesterday) is fast coming apart. Technology is changing so rapidly that equipment formerly enjoying a 30-year life cycle is becoming obsolete*

> *almost as fast as it is installed. As quickly as new technology creates new products, customers everywhere want a wider choice of telecommunication services ...The stakes in this new global battle are enormous."*

The computer is also making its presence known in outer space. New computer technology and laser breakthroughs have influenced our government to make plans for war in the heavens. An item in the April 1984 bulletin of The Research Institute of America; is headlined: "A Year Closer To Star Wars Defense — Pentagon and high-tech planners have pushed ahead with President Reagan's controversial 'Star Wars' missile defense system."

On the domestic scene there appears no limit to the growing dependence on computers. An article on page 80 of the science magazine *Discover* for May 1984 reports on growing computerized dating and marriage services. A news story in the April 1, 1984 *Norman Transcript* published in Norman, Oklahoma, reports on how computers perfectly match the opposite sexes. The article is titled, "Boy Meets Girl — Can Modern Technology Help Romances Bloom?"

> *"The Fourth Generation computer age was made possible by the discovery and/or invention of the silicon computer chip which is made from quartz or sand. However, the silicon chip has no defense against outside power sources. Even lightning will burn a silicon chip to a crisp, and it is theorized that a single 50-megaton air blast over Chicago would knock out every single computer in the United States and Canada.*

"However, the next generation of computers will have biochips, and these will actually repel outside interference and would be destroyed only by a close atomic blast." We quote from the December 1983 edition of United Airline *magazine: "... if you took all the information in all the computers existing in the world today, and used biomolecular technology, it would fit into one sugar cube ... one could squeeze about one billion times the amount of circuitry into a biochip as into one of today's conventional silicon computer chips."*

According to the article, biochips are made from antibodies that are prevalent in the human body that fight disease germs. These antibodies have only a short life span, but through an induced fusion between them and cancer cells, the result is ... a wildly reproducing cancer cell (which) results in a unique inheritance: an immortal hybrid cell, or hybridoma, that eternally manufactures antibodies, one after another, each identical.

The Fifth Generation computer will, in effect, be a living entity. It will reproduce itself and program itself, and theoretically, one super computer could indeed control the total activities of every human being on planet Earth.

Will the Antichrist attempt to create a new generation of immortal computerized human beings? It appears that Bible prophecy in this regard is very similar to that envisioned by Dr. Jastrow and others.

In the *Iliad,* Homer wrote that the god Hephaestus made splendid robots to relieve the gods and goddesses of mundane chores in looking after the human race. We know from Genesis 6 that much of mythology is based on the true accounts of Satan's effort to subvert God's creation, man, and claim the earth for himself. Perhaps the Fifth Generation computer will be another attempt.

In any event, scientists are now working feverishly to fulfill man's demand for bigger, better and more intelligent computers, and God has said, what man has imagined, that he can do. But there is one thing no computer can do for man. We quote from the article "Computer Worship" that appears in the May 1984 edition of *Science* magazine:

> *"Massachusetts Institute of Technology computer scientist Joseph Weizenbaum suggests, 'Take the great many people who've dealt with computers now for a long time ... and ask whether they're in any better position to solve life's problems. And I think the answer is clearly no. They're just as confused and mixed up about the world and their personal relations and so on as anyone else.' "*

4
COMPUTER NETWORKS

A foreshadowing of universal economics by a central authority control, probably by the Common Market, was seen in an article titled "A World Information War" that appeared in the February 1978 edition of the official magazine of the Common Market, *European Community:*

> "At least one expert sees the world on the verge of an 'information cold war,' whose first skirmishes are already being heard in Europe, the United Nations, and a sampling of national legislatures. To understand the shadowy issues wrought by the information, one must first understand how computer networks work. Computers not only compute; they can also store information — vast quantities of it — They can be queried from a distance — from the moon if necessary ... Data banks have multiplied — more in the United States than elsewhere, though Europe has been striving mightily to catch up — The technology is

> *perfect for international use ... In the United States the number of computer queries increased tenfold in three years; Europe's are expected to double to 4 million between 1980 and 1985. This demand occasioned the creation of Euronet, a major international network of scientific and technological data banks that is to be in full operation in December 1978. When complete, Euronet will link more than 100 data banks ... Eventually Euronet is to include data on textiles, engineering, socio-economics, chemistry, agriculture, medicine, legislation, electronics, physics, environment, aerospace, metallurgy, nucleonics, and patents."*

To demonstrate how the Common Market countries of Europe are getting into communications and satellite computer networks in a big way; as they unknowingly weave the framework for the Antichrist system, we refer to *Europe* Magazine, May-June 1985 edition, page 24:

> *"The European Community is poised on the starting line of a RACE against time. RACE is in capital letters, because it's the name of a breathtakingly ambitious, hugely expensive, plan to catapult Europe into the front rank of telecommunications technology. If it wins national government backing, it will mean a $100-billion-plus project to transform a splintered, inefficient and old-fashioned telecommunications network into the finest on earth.*

COMPUTER NETWORKS 49

"Already, the E.C. Commission has unveiled plans for a 10-year program to introduce integrated broadband communications throughout the community. That's jargon for a high-speed electronic system capable of carrying mind-boggling quantities of information in the form of reproduced documents, video pictures and computer conversations, as well as the dear old human voice.

"The new system would employ sophisticated digital switching, glass-fiber optical cables and satellite transmission. It will put the present jumble of copper-cable, low-speed, nationally run telephone networks squarely in the technological steam age. The Commission's blueprint involves an initial research program of about $30 million. The E.C. will shoulder slightly more than half the cost, the rest being met by companies contributing to the research — and expecting a share in the ultimate rewards.

"After 18 months, the Commission reckons, the main RACE program could start. The first phase would run from 1986 to 1991, involving field trials through to development of the technology base. The second phase, from 1991 to 1996, would see the progressive construction of the space-age system."

Concerning the latest advance in the international computer banking service of SWIFT, we refer to the October 19, 1982 edition of *Solutions,* a Burroughs publication:

> "In the time that it takes you to write a check and hand it to the cashier at the supermarket, you can send ten million dollars from New York to Hong Kong with flawless accuracy and a very high level of security, at any time of night or day. But you'll need help — from SWIFT, the Society for Worldwide Interbank Financial Telecommunications. SWIFT is a non-profit cooperative society — but it is far more than that. SWIFT is the world's largest and most sophisticated interbank payment system. It is the long-needed medium for the standardization of transaction messages. It is the provider of an essential — and potentially vast — array of services. Finally, it is a state-of-the-art computer and telecommunications network that interfaces with over a thousand banks, encompasses five continents, and handles over 340,000 transactions each day with reliability that is very close to 100 percent ... In its simplest version, a bank SWIFT interface consists of a mini-computer linked to the terminals through which messages are keyed into the network. With the appropriate displays on the computer's display screen, the software guides the operator, from sign-on to correct message entry ... Security at the bank SWIFT interfaces is largely up to the banks ... But just as a telephone company cannot be held responsible for what is said over its

lines, SWIFT cannot be concerned with policing the premises of 1,000-odd banks ... Further down the road lie some intriguing possibilities — the generation of processing of text; voice transmission ... image transmission ... on-line data base inquiry ... In the marketing realm, SWIFT is already offering its own interface device and may someday market a terminal for credit card verification — or even its own encryption device ... SWIFT is a corp of exceedingly able and dedicated people presiding over an immensely complex collection of electronic technology. But it has become more than either of those — and perhaps even more than the sum of the two. Its success is due in large part to the effort and determination of Carl Reuterskiold, General Manager of SWIFT, and his staff. But there is an idealism operating as well. 'We're very conscious,' says Zabell, 'that there's a chance to do something unusual. There's not likely to be many SWIFT's ever.' And the hints at another explanation for why SWIFT has become what it is: SWIFT is the realization of a deep human yearning for universality. As such, it is significant achievement in our search for ways to surmount the barrier that we ourselves have created."

The letters for SWIFT stand for Society for Worldwide Interbank Financial Telecommunications. It is a non-profit organization representing 1,000 banks on five continents. Its primary function, or service, is electronic fund transfer (EFT). SWIFT will be able to provide voice transmission, image transmissions, and multiple computer banking services, including individual credit card transaction, credit information, and personal data on anyone whose number is in the various data banks around the world. SWIFT I was replaced by SWIFT II in 1984 and extends to 1986. The secondary purpose of SWIFT as a non-profit organization is idealistic and humanistic — in a religious sense, to satisfy the "deep human yearning ...." to become as one with all men in universality. SWIFT will interface with any common computer system, including mini-computers and micro-computers. SWIFT insists that international computer banking and business will be almost 100 percent safe, yet the society does *not* guarantee that it will be absolutely 100 percent safe. A September edition of *Christian Science Monitor* reads:

> *"The industrial world is rushing headlong to replace letters, receipts and currency with electronic impulses in computer networks. And as it does, some experts warn that without proper safeguards, these networks may become increasingly vulnerable to manipulation by political extremists or foreign powers. 'We, as a nation and as a world, are charging merrily ahead with the process of computerization without really looking at what we are doing',' warned Willis Ware of the Rand Corporation. Computer crime expert Donn P. Parker of SRI International said, for example, that unless proper safeguards are taken, growing dependence on electronic funds transfer*

(EFT) systems will increase the risk that extremists or foreign agents can tamper with them ... 'The physical or logical destruction of (such a system) which could, in turn cause economic collapse of a country, is a more appealing and cost effective form of war than one using nuclear bombs and missiles ... ' Parker said ... A single large commercial bank will transfer from $30 billion to $60 billion a day by computer. The network that ties together members in the U.S. Federal Reserve turns over an amount equal to the national debt every four days ... The most serious threat to the nation's security posed by this process would be the covert destruction of large amounts of the electronic or 'virtual' money. This could be accomplished by erasing all record of it from the computers involved, Parker said. If $160 billion were obliterated in this fashion, it could create an economic catastrophe, he said."

The elimination of all forms of money and checks in favor of international electronic funds transfer is a certainty. But once this electronic international banking system is established and in operation, computer experts warn that a small international conspiracy could create world economic chaos and take over the entire system.

Cashless electronic banking is already being put to the test and has emerged decidedly successful. Quoting the *Midland Reporter-Telegram,* October 28, 1984, an article entitled "Bank Operates Well Without Cash Hassles":

"Lone Star National Bank is like any new banking enterprise. Its officers work hard to drum up deposits, its tellers are courteous, and lines are short. But it lacks something most others have — cash. Originally, when its chairman decided to operate without cash, the idea was to do it only while the bank was housed in temporary quarters. But two months after opening the doors, Lone Star's executives like the way things are going so much that they have decided the time has come for a cashless, completely electronic bank.

" 'We're growing at a nice rate and we're not running into customer resistance, so we plan to continue operating without cash,' said Joe Stedman, chairman and chief executive officer of the bank.

"Sheldon D. Golub, a spokesman for the American Bankers Association, said he knew of no other bank in the nation working without cash. Lone Star, with $6 million in assets and 150 depositors, has more than doubled its assets since opening August 3, 1984 in an industrial area near downtown, catering to medium-size businesses. The small bank's two tellers do not accept cash deposits, do not make cash withdrawals and do not cash employee paychecks. Most transactions are done by mail. If customers want cash, they must use automatic teller machines."

COMPUTER NETWORKS

The Smart Card that will probably be much in evidence within 18 months will make cash passé and computer banking very popular. Quoting from the *Daytona Beach Morning Journal,* May 10, 1985, entitled "The Smart Card — Built-In Computer Knows Your Limit":

"Will there be computers in your wallet soon? Blue Cross and Blue Shield of Maryland announced earlier this week that 1.6 million customers would receive laser 'LifeCards' during the next two years. Like video discs and compact audio discs, the wallet-size membership cards store information — up to 800 pages of medical history, including X-rays and electrocardiograms.

This summer, thousands of MasterCard customers in south Florida will receive 'smart' credit cards that contain tiny computer microprocessors. In 200 stores equipped with terminals to handle them, customers won't have to wait for a credit check. The information is stored right in the card, and so is a record of their transactions, which is updated every time they make a purchase. Eventually, the LifeCard system could be made available to Blue Cross and Blue Shield companies nationwide. And if MasterCard adopts the Smart Card, it would mean millions of people will be carrying computers in their wallets. Robert Kitchener, president of Casio Microcards Inc., which is providing 50,000 cards and 200 machines for the MasterCard test, predicted that Smart

Cards will be widespread in the United States in two years."

Ultimately there will be a universal credit card in preparation for the universal number (see Rev. 13:16, 17) to follow. In fact, such a universal card is already being considered under the caption "Moneytalk" in the *USA Today,* September 12, 1984. "Universal card gains acceptance":

> *"If you like the idea of a universal bank card that can be used in place of cash or to tap a credit line, you'll be happy to know many more USA banks and merchants are jumping into POS — retail 'point-of-sale' debit card experiments. The ultimate goal of POS is to replace paper transactions with electronic transfer of funds from your bank account to a merchant's.*
>
> *"Officials from Exxon Corp., and Montgomery Ward gave their views of POS potential at the National Bank Card Conference in Washington, D.C. Monday. VISA U.S.A. has announced a new generation of terminals to be used in a Cincinnati pilot program to 'read' plastic cards for POS transactions. And CIRRUS, a nationwide network of automated teller machines, recently announced plans to expand into POS: Its ATM cards will be usable in place of cash at many retail outlets in 1985."*

We can already see the handwriting on the wall, or should we say, on the computer screen. If you have not made your peace with God and believed on Jesus Christ as your personal Savior, do so, this very hour.

"Now then we are ambassadors for Christ, as though God did beseech you by us: we pray you in Christ's stead, be ye reconciled to God. For he hath made him to be sin for us, who knew no sin; that we might be made the righteousness of God in him." (2 Corinthians 5:20, 21).

5
COMPUTER SPIES

According to Scripture, God is omnipotent (all powerful), omniscient (all knowing) and omnipresent (present everywhere). It is by God's power that all things were created and by which all things consist. In the popular movie of 1977, *Star Wars,* two forces in the universe were set forth. The "good force" being the motivation for righteousness, and the "evil force" the instigator of all that is bad.

While we in no way endorse this movie as a guide for morality, the producers may have unknowingly depicted the coming struggle between God and His angels, and Satan and his angelic force (Revelation 12). In *Star Wars* men and spirits were fighting in outer space where computerized machines were fighting alongside human combatants.

The Bible, human history, and even the conscience of man, give proof that there are two forces at war in the universe. These two forces are diametrically opposed to each other. But more than just forces, the two opponents are living personalities. According to Scripture, God is the force for good; the devil is the force for evil.

In Ezekiel 28:13-18 we read that an "anointed cherub" in God's government conceived ideas in his mind that he could become greater than his Creator. That he was an "anointed" or "crowned" angelic being signified that he had been given governmental authority. This particular cherub was more beautiful than all others, and God had given him great wisdom. The specific charge against this high angelic prince is listed in Ezekiel 28:17, "Thine heart was lifted up because of thy beauty, thou has corrupted thy wisdom by reason of thy brightness ... "

The ambitions of this "anointed cherub" to whom God had given a kingdom are identified in Isaiah 14:12-14, "How art thou fallen from heaven, O Lucifer, son of the morning! how art thou cut down to the ground, which didst weaken the nations! For thou hast said in thine heart, I will ascend into heaven, I will exalt my throne above the stars of God ... I will be like the most High."

The Kingdom of God is a literal government of order and purpose. The Earth is a rebel planet in God's Kingdom. Christians are citizens of the Kingdom of God living in enemy territory until Jesus Christ returns to bring the Earth back into His Kingdom.

We are given some insight into the administrative composition of the government of God in Revelation 4:2-4, 6-7 " ... a throne was set in heaven, and one sat on the throne. And he that sat was to look upon like a jasper and a sardine stone: and there was a rainbow round about the throne ... And round about the throne were four and twenty seats: and upon the seats I saw four and twenty elders sitting, clothed in white raiment; and they had on their heads crowns of gold ... and round about the throne, were four beasts full of eyes before and behind. And the first beast was like a lion, and the second beast like a calf, and the third beast had a face as a man, and the fourth beast was like a flying eagle ... "

It is evident from the biblical description of God's throne, meaning His central government, that from the beginning God delegated authority just as judges sit upon benches today, or senators hold seats in the legislative branch of our federal government. Also, the 24 elders before God's throne wear crowns, symbolizing governmental authority. The number 24 is the sum of two times 12 (two the number of witnesses and 12 the number of government). The four beasts derive their names from the Greek word *zoe*, having reference to "zoo, the animal creation." The fact that they are full of eyes and rest not day nor night signifies that they are watchers, or as we would say today, observers, or even spies. There is nothing that happens in the whole creation that escapes the attention of God. The psalmist wrote that although he would try to hide himself in the earth, or ascend into heaven, God would be there.

The kingdom of Babylon came under observation by God's angelic observers because of the authority it exercised over a large part of the earth. We read the words of the prophet concerning the surveillance of Nebuchadnezzar's kingdom in Daniel 4:13, "I saw in the visions of my head ... and, behold, a watcher and an holy one came down from heaven." We read of the judgment passed upon Nebuchadnezzar for his own selfish, satanically inspired pride, in glorifying himself above the Creator in Daniel 4:17: "This matter is by the decree of the watchers, and the demand by the word of the holy ones: to the intent that the living may know that the most High ruleth in the kingdom of men, and giveth it to whomsoever he will, and setteth up over it the basest of men."

It is apparent from the context that the four watchers reported to the heavenly senate of the 24 Holy Ones the abuse of governmental authority by Nebuchadnezzar. Then, one watcher and one Holy One came down from heaven to carry out a predetermined judgment. Subsequently, Nebuchadnezzar's kingdom was taken from him for seven years.

Satan is today still trying to exalt his throne above the stars of God. Man, not angels, was made in the image of God, and what man can imagine, that he can do (Gen. 11:6). In attempting to counterfeit the Kingdom of God, thus maintaining the creation, Satan needs the imaginative powers of man.

John Wesley White made an interesting observation on page 35 of his book *World War III* when he states: "The Bible tells us that 'man looketh on the outward appearance, but the Lord looketh on the heart' (I Sam. 16:7). God says this. Man is now capable of looking out into the universe through a radio-telescope nearly two miles long in the Netherlands, or through one with a face a thousand feet in diameter in Puerto Rico, capable of spotting a postage stamp on the moon. If this is true, what can't Christ, at His coming, see in the human heart when nothing ... is hidden from God's sight? Everything is uncovered and laid bare before the eyes of Him to whom we must give account (Heb. 4:13). The Chinese recently launched into orbit a series of sophisticated spy satellites from their desert in Inner Mongolia. With these satellites they can monitor minute details of life in the Soviet Union and the United States in particular, and the rest of the world in general. Both Russia and the United States have a network of 'spy-in-the-sky' satellites that on a clear day can allegedly count the number of potato hills in your garden, or even, when you are sitting on a lawn chair, read your newspaper over your shoulder."

According to the May 7, 1978 edition of *Parade,* since October of 1957, more than 10,500 spacecraft have been put into orbit by 14 nations. The activities of almost every person on earth are being monitored somehow by a spy in outer space. Also, the use of computerized, orbiting satellites to control the thinking of men and women, even to the point of getting them to worship some individual as God, or even influence their national allegiance, is a real possibility. A UPI release that appeared in the November 11, 1974 edition of *The Wichita Eagle* stated in part:

> *"Satellites orbiting the earth can beam messages directly to television sets in viewers' homes to brainwash people without them even knowing it, according to a United Nations report. By sending out so-called subliminal messages that are recorded only in viewers' subconscious, the technique can be used to mass-hypnotize and influence policies of other countries ... "*

To demonstrate how the computer is rapidly becoming indispensible to every area of life, and how new computer technologies are enabling certain organizations to far outstrip their rivals, consider the cover story of *Business Week,* October 14, 1985 entitled "Information Power," page 108:

> *"For all the talk about the Information Age, most computers are still just workhorses — churning out payrolls, reports, numerical analyses. But slowly, stealthily, companies are turning their machines into a lot more ...*
>
> *"**Fresh Mind-Set.** In part, the change simply reflects the proliferation of computers. But there's more to it than that. Information technologies are reaching a critical mass. Business is beginning to reconfigure things from the ground up — this time with the computers in mind. The result: entirely different approaches to existing markets and whole new product lines that didn't seem a logical extension of the business before. Retailer J.C. Penney now processes credit card transactions for Shell Oil and Gulf Refining & Marketing as a way to leverage its investment in its information network. Who would have foreseen such relationships 10 years ago?*
>
> *"At the same time, computers, telecommunications, and video technology are merging into something bigger and better than the individual components. What is a telecommu-nications system these days without a computer? As the technologies become more entwined, the potentials of each suddenly multiply. And as they become part of everyday life, more people*

are perceiving new ways to use them. What becomes essential is a fresh mind-set, a new way of perceiving the role of information technology in business.

"The ability to use computers and telecom-munications creatively to collect, make sense of, and distribute information is already spelling the difference between success and mediocrity in industries ranging from banking to bicycle making, at companies as large as General Motors Corp., and as small as automobile body shops ...

"Consider three classic cases, mythologized in Harvard Business School case studies and preached with evangelical fervor by a growing cadre of information management experts:

"• Merrill Lynch & Co. used computers to create one of its most successful new products ever: the Cash Management Account. By combining information on a customer's checking, savings, credit card, and securities accounts into one computerized monthly statement and automatically 'sweeping' idle funds into interest-bearing money market funds, Merrill Lynch has lured billions of dollars of assets from other places since it introduced CMA in 1978. It now manages $85 billion. And though rivals eventually concocted similar offerings, it still has almost 70 percent of the market.

"• American Hospital Supply Corp., which distributes products from 8,500

manufacturers to more than 100,000 health care providers, saw its market share soar in the 1970s after it set up computer links to its customers and suppliers.

"• American Airlines Inc. has used computer and communications technology to build an entirely new business with sky-high profit margins. American provides its Sabre reservation system, which lists the flight schedules of every major airline in the world, to 48 percent of the approximately 24,000 automated travel agents in the U.S. They pay American $1.75 for every reservation made via Sabre for other carriers. American's parent, AMR Corp., which earned $400 million pretax last year on $5.3 billion in revenues, expects Sabre alone to earn it $170 million before taxes this year on $388 million in revenues. 'We are now in the data processing as well as the airline business,' says President Robert L. Crandall, a data processing expert who conceived Sabre a decade ago, when he was American's marketing chief.

"Such success stories have sent companies in every industry scrambling to find ways to harness the power of information technology — from computers and telephones to commu-nications satellites and video-disks."

We readily begin to see how the vast telecommunica-tion systems of all nations will serve the demands of Antichrist, the final world ruler, via satellite and the amazing computer. The awesome prophetic picture is becoming more sharply etched on the computer images of the future.

In the book of Revelation we read that an image, or we might say today, a machine, will speak to everyone in the world, and command all the inhabitants to worship the Antichrist as God.

This will be Satan's effort to duplicate God's omnipresence. In the field of computer science today, it is rapidly becoming possible for everyone to have his own omnipresent guide and counselor, the friendly talking computer. We read of this modern Paraclete of computer science in the October 1980 edition of *Discover:*

> *"Computers that speak seem no more out of the ordinary nowadays than talking pictures. But while most voice computers are preprogrammed with only about 200 words and phrases, Votrax, produced by the Votrax Company of Troy, Michigan, has a virtually limitless vocabulary. It is a tiny, $12 computer chip that will fit into a hand-held affair, much like a pocket calculator, and will speak for people who cannot."*

Also consider projections for a world computer by *Globescan,* July 20, 1985:

> *"Economic Planning: the World Computer: The power to control every person on earth, all buying and selling now being achieved ...*

Globescan comment:

COMPUTER SPIES

> "The new IRS computer in Martinsburg, West Virginia, will contain a profile on each citizen so detailed that it will help the world computer to control the buying and selling of every person on earth. That's an awesome thought."

We further consider the issue between privacy and technology as detailed in the *Daily News Digest*, July 24, 1985:

> "Americans have become increasingly concerned that our Federal Big Brother is ever more nosy concerning every activity of law-abiding citizens. One of the better-known examples is the federal requirement that virtually every private financial transaction be recorded, along with the ID number of the citizens involved, even in cases where no possible tax liability can be involved.
>
> "A less well-known area of potential personal privacy violations is that of communications. The courts have held that the government has every right to know all about one's telephone communications, especially when cordless phones are used, and new potential problems lie in the areas of cable TV service and mobile telephone systems.
>
> "In the case of cable TV, the records of the TV firm will soon (if they don't already) contain extensive information about the viewing habits of individual families. And where security services are hooked into the

> cable system, the records can even show the comings and goings of family members! Such records, of course, are readily available to snoopy government investigators.
>
> "Cellular mobile-phone systems have the capability (and will soon be offering) tracking services; the location of any given mobile phone can be tracked to an accuracy of better than 100 feet. Such a technique can be quite useful in finding stolen vehicles, but also will allow Big Brother to keep track of thee and me — without our being aware of it. Thus, Big Brother will be able to monitor where we go and who our associates are — all recorded and analyzed by computers."

We refer to the role the False Prophet, the head of the coming World Church, will play when Antichrist comes to power:

> "And he had power to give life unto the image of the beast, that the image of the beast should both speak, and cause that as many as would not worship the image of the beast should be killed. And he causeth all, both small and great, rich and poor, free and bond, to receive a mark in their right hand, or in their foreheads: And that no man might buy or sell, save he that had the mark, or the name of the beast, or the number of his name" (Rev. 13:15-17).

Comparing the rapid turn of world events today with biblical prophecy is more thrilling than reading the best-seller in fictional books. Satan, through man, finally does have almost god-like omnipresent power. Satan is making his final push to exalt his throne above the stars of God.

6
COMPUTER OVER BEAST

As our modern society has become more dependent upon the computer, instead of man retaining dominion over the animal kingdom, the computer has been steadily taking over this responsibility. The population explosion has resulted in the destruction of many of the natural habitats of wildlife, and man's own greed has caused the complete extinction of some species. These factors have contributed to the increased computer control of fish, fowl and animal life.

The Bible states in Genesis 1, verses 28 and 29, that when God gave man dominion over all fish, fowl and beasts, He forbade the eating of any flesh. Instead, God pointed man to the herbs, fruits, and nuts, and He told Adam and Eve that this would be their meat. The word for meat used here in the Hebrew means "protein," and Josephus explained that before the Flood the plants were so rich in food value that the flesh of animals was not needed. God cursed the ground after the first man and the first woman sinned. However, even then man still had communion with the animals. Adam, at the first,

COMPUTER OVER BEAST

named the animals, and there was no fear between men and beasts. We believe there was some kind of communication between men and animals.

The Scriptures do indicate that it will be possible for man to once more communicate with the animals when Jesus Christ returns to this earth. We read of this golden age in Isaiah 11:6-9:

> *"The wolf also shall dwell with the lamb, and the leopard shall lie down with the kid; and the calf and the young lion and fatling together, and a little child shall lead them. And the cow and the bear shall feed; their young ones shall lie down together: and the lion shall eat straw like the ox. And the sucking child shall play on the hole of the asp, and the weaned child shall put his hand on the cockatrice den. They shall not hurt nor destroy in all my holy mountain: for the earth shall be full of the knowledge of the Lord, as the waters cover the sea."*

Charles Darwin saw animals eating each other and called it a part of evolution, the survival of the fittest. The Bible says it is a result of sin. God spoke to Noah after He had cursed the earth a second time because of sin in Genesis 9:2-3:

> *"And the fear of you and the dread of you shall be upon every beast of the earth, and upon every fowl of the air, upon all that moveth upon the earth, and upon all the fishes of the sea; into your hand are they delivered. Every moving thing that liveth*

> *shall be meat for you; even as the green herb have I given you all things."*

It was evidently at this time that man first killed animals to obtain protein, and animals began to eat each other. But the promise of God is that this curse will be removed when Jesus Christ returns to put down sin and rebellion. This biblical prophecy is also recorded in Romans 8:18-22:

> *"For I reckon that the sufferings of this present time are not worthy to be compared with the glory which shall be revealed in us. For the earnest expectation of the creature waiteth for the manifestation of the sons of God. For the creature was made subject to vanity, not willingly, but by reason of him who hath subjected the same in hope. Because the creature itself also shall be delivered from the bondage of corruption into the glorious liberty of the children of God. For we know that the whole creation groaneth and travaileth in pain together until now."*

Jesus Christ died for the sins of *whosoever* would believe on Him, and because Christ died for sin, creation will be delivered from the curse of sin. God is concerned about everything He created, even the birds, and the lilies and the grass that grows in our yards (Luke 12:22-28). God's promise to the creation is that it will be delivered from the curse of sin — droughts, storms, frosts and the other environmental factors that prevent the plant and animal kingdoms from fulfilling the complete will and purpose of God in creation. But even today the fowls of the air, the beasts of the forest, and the fish in rivers, lakes and oceans are under angelic observation, and a sparrow's falling does not escape the attention of God. The animal-like appearance of the heavenly watchers perhaps signifies the divisions of the living creation over which they continually observe (Rev. 4:6-11).

Of Jesus Christ, by whom the Father created all things, we read in Colossians 1:13-17:

> "Who hath delivered us from the power of darkness (the power of Satan), and hath translated us into the kingdom of his dear Son: In whom we have redemption through his blood, even the forgiveness of sins: Who is the image of the invisible God, the firstborn of every creature: For by him were all things created, that are in heaven, and that are in earth, visible and invisible, whether they be thrones, or dominions, or principalities, or powers: all things were created by him, and for him: and he is before all things, and by him all things consist."

Satan will soon make a final attempt to exalt his throne above the stars of God (Rev. 12), and this master plan of the devil includes setting up his own false messiah, the Antichrist, over the dominion of planet Earth. But how can Satan's plan duplicate God's provisions and sustaining power over the creation? Concerning this intriguing question, an interesting article appeared in *The Sunday Oklahoman,* December 29, 1974 edition, under the heading, "Chimpanzee Talks to Scientists Through Use of Computer Language":

> *"Dr. Geoffrey Bourne lifted a blue tennis shoe and tapped it against the window of a Plexiglas and steel cage. Inside, a four-year-old chimpanzee peered out. 'Come on, Lana. Say something,' Bourne whispered ... He began waving the shoe in front of the chimpanzee. Lana gave a long sigh ... and then padded over to a large keyboard ... With furry fingers, she pushed four squares ... a teletype converted the message into English. The message read, ... 'Shoe name of this (it's blue)' ... Chimps don't have the necessary vocal cords so the scientists taught Lana a computer language they call 'yerkish.' Lana can punch messages out on machines inside or outside her cage. For the sake of visitors and a scientific record, all messages are recorded in English by an automatic printer. 'Lana loves coffee' (her trainer said) as he moved into her cage area with a steaming cup from his office ... Lana moved to her talking machine ... studied the machine for a moment (and the words came) 'you give cup of coffee ... Tim give Lana this can.'"*

This is a charming, true story illustrating that whatever man can imagine, he can do. The words of the song, "If We Could Talk With the Animals," are seemingly coming to pass. Through computers man can again talk with the animals and the animals can talk with man. However, we must remember that the

COMPUTER OVER BEAST

interrupting of communications between man and the animals was a restriction placed by God because of the sin problem and a condition that was not to be resolved until the return of Jesus Christ. Therefore, we must conclude that this is just one more example of how the knowledge explosion is encouraging man to cast off the bonds established by God. The Scriptures indicate that Satan will use such knowledge to attempt to establish his evil kingdom upon the earth.

Another related article in the same edition of *The Sunday Oklahoman* was carried under the heading, "When It Comes to Measuring a Racehorse, Odds Favor The Computer":

> *"An Oklahoman measures physically on the outside and electronically on the inside. And the next result is that, barring any human or equine error, he can pick the finishers with mathematical probability — provided all were 'measured', ... eight horses measured were entered in a race. Except for error when numbers five and six bumped each other, they finished in exactly the order predicted. Since then, as many as 10 horses have been measured in a single race on several occasions and have finished one through 10 the way the computer analysis predicted ..."*

This article continues to relate how computers are being used to gauge animals in racing for gambling purposes. Therefore, we wonder how well animals will relate to man when man is determined to use them for evil purposes. That the whole creation, being the result of a creative act by a righteous God, is by nature against sin is self-evident (Romans 8). Nature on earth travails because of sin in the human heart. Thus, we must consider the possibility that the use of the computer to spy out God's secrets and control the animal world may be the reason that the animals and the fowls will rebel when iniquity on earth reaches its peak during the Tribulation. We read of this time in Revelation 6:8, "And I looked, and behold a pale horse: and his name that sat on him was Death, and Hell followed with him. And power was given unto them over the fourth part of the earth, to kill with sword, and with hunger, and with death, and with the BEASTS OF THE EARTH."

It was also noted by the apostle John in Revelation 19:17-21 that the fowls of the whole earth will gather at the Battle of Armageddon. At this battle the armies of Antichrist will be composed of the most sinful men who ever lived, complete rebels against God, and the fowls will gather there in great numbers to eat the flesh of this great army.

Branding livestock with the owner's identifying brand to prove ownership dates back thousands of years. As we have previously brought out, the Babylonian system is depicted as a type of the coming kingdom of Antichrist. The power of Nebuchadnezzar extended over even the animals as we are informed in Daniel 2:37, 38,

> "Thou, O king, art a king of kings: for the God of heaven hath given thee a kingdom, power, and strength, and glory. And wheresoever the children of men dwell, the

> *beasts of the field and the fowls of the heaven hath he given into thine hand, and hath made thee ruler over them all ... "*

Nebuchadnezzar was the avenger of God to execute judgment, but God was always in strict control. God also allowed the king authority and power to demonstrate a prophetic teaching. It is quite possible that the beasts in Babylon were marked with a symbol of ownership and for a purpose. In recent years the marking of animals for identification purposes has gained wide acceptance. An article in the March 11, 1966 edition of *The Evening Times* states in part:

> *"Dr. David H. Timrud, a physician at the University's McCosh Infirmary (Princeton Univer-sity), has given both time and money towards the establishment of a National Dog Registry ... Dog thieves, by removing tags immediately, have turned dognapping into a lucrative business by selling the forsaken animals to medical research laboratories. Dr. Timrud proposes that dogs be tattooed on the right groin with the owner's Social Security number ... the number ... would then be reported to the National Dog Registry."*

Dr. R. Keith Farrell of Washington State University is an aggressive exponent of universal animal-marking. Dr. Farrell has perfected a laser tattoo numbering gun that will number fish swimming in water in one-billionth of a second. Concerning the numbering of animals, Dr. Farrell stated in a Horse Identification Seminar:

> "We have proposed a breed or state registry, year of birth, and an individual six-digit number. This system using the freeze-making technique, has recently been accepted by the Arabian Registry for official registry identification."

Dr. Farrell continued to state that "These marks should be a permanent part of the animal and be exclusive to that individual." In other words, Dr. Farrell means that it would be possible to mark every animal in the world with a mark to be interpreted in six digits — the breed, age and registration number of any animal. Such markings tied to computer control have been done on experimental mice, and the code-marking system itself is already in wide use for domesticated animals. If such code marks can be applied to animals for police control, so can it be applied to human beings for the same reason.

God gave to Nebuchadnezzar the authority to claim dominion over every animal in the world. Of course, Nebuchadnezzar never attained this height of power over the animal kingdom. Nevertheless, the Antichrist will try again and the technical capability through computerized markings and transponders make it possible. Through such sophisticated devices, it is even possible to track flies with a special Dopler radar process. This was reported by the University of California in an experiment at the Los Alamos Scientific Laboratory.

The Washington Farmer-Stockman of June 2, 1977 reported the laser and radar warning systems

COMPUTER OVER BEAST

to track insect pests to be destroyed are being set up. In our generation there has developed a great public concern about animals on the endangered species lists. A NASA release of January 1970 stated in part:

> "In 1966, at the Smithsonian Institution in Washington, D.C., a special meeting was called between leading ecologists to discuss the feasibility and practicability of tracking a wide variety of animals from orbiting spacecraft ... some birds such as ospreys and others could also be tracked by satellites."

In the Millennium, the curse upon the plant and animal kingdoms because of sin, will be removed. According to Isaiah and other prophets, the lion will lie down with the lamb and children can play with poisonous reptiles. Concerning vegetation, the deserts will blossom as a rose. Satan must attempt to duplicate this feature of the Millennium. The technology is now available to counterfeit these promises of God.

From Peter Lalonde's recent *Prophecy Newsletter* comes the startling information that Identification Devices Inc. of Westminister, Colorado, can now provide minitransponders to be implanted under the skin of your pet (cat or dog) as a permanent identification means.

Quoting from the *Prophecy Newsletter's* article "The Mark of the Beast is Now Being Tested!" says:

> "If you refuse to allow your cat to wear an identification collar because of the possibility the collar might get caught on something

and hang the cat, you might be interested in this new method of Identification Devices Inc. It's an ultrathin microchip, which a veterinarian will inject under the cat's skin. The microchip emits a numerical or letter combination code (about 3 to 4 billion are possible), which is assigned exclusively to that cat ... Its inventors believe that the widespread use of this technique of permanent identification could help save some of the thousands of animals."

But experimentation on humans as well as fish, race horses, and pets is also being done. Reproduced verbatim, is a portion of the System I. D. Promotional Packet:

"Combine some of the most exciting developments in advanced technology and here's what you get: an identification system of almost unlimited versatility. 'Suppose you were to make a list of the technical advances that are quickly reshaping the way we live: microminiaturization of electronic components. High-speed data processing system, powerful new computer-programming techniques, extremely sophisticated telecommunications devices, and new methods of encapsulating delicate components so they can function in unfavorable environments. Then consider how these innovations might be employed to solve the age-old problem of providing positive identification of people, animals and equipment. That's what the design

specialists at Identification Devices did. And here's the result:

"Fish biologists now can easily identify and track the movements of large numbers of fish moving past a given point. A microminiature transponder implanted in the target fish transmits each fish's identification number upon command. This information is automatically displayed, printed, or recorded for future analysis. Meanwhile, the implanted device has no adverse effect on the fish.

"Similarly, race horses entering the paddock area at a racetrack can be checked automatically to verify their identities and to record certain physiological conditions.

"Employees working on restricted projects have this same type of transponder embedded in a tamper-proof badge. The unique identification signal emitted by the device upon command permits access to secured areas. It is also used to automatically log each person's movements in and out of restricted areas. Should unauthorized entry be attempted, the system immediately alerts security personnel.

"And at a federal laboratory in New Mexico, access to top-secret rooms is controlled by a device that focuses on the blood vessels behind the eye. But, despite the controversy surrounding such attempts, researchers are exploring signature dynamics — machines that analyze how you sign your name, not the actual signature, but brainwaves and even typing rhythms."

Peter Lalonde also gives a quick review of six reasons why these electronic transponders are just as adaptable and even more feasible for humans than for animals.

> "*A Quick Review — Identification Devices claim that 'these innovations might be employed to solve the age-old problem of providing positive identification of people ...'*
>
> "• *Employees working on restricted projects already have these chips planted in tamper-proof badges.*
>
> "• *Chips are already being tested in the flesh of horses, fish and cats.*
>
> "• *Transponders can generate 4 billion unique numbers — while the world population is now about 4 billion people.*
>
> "• *Operating life of the chip is 100 years which is the maximum anticipated lifespan of a human, not a horse, fish or cat.*
>
> "• *Identification Devices boasts the capacity to handle a network of 1 million terminals — a 'few' more than necessary to coordinate the tracking of horses, fish and cats.*"

This exciting and technical evidence indicates that the world is getting ready for the mark of the Beast.

Whether the evolving control system of marking animals is called "computer over beast" or something else, the Bible indicates it may one day provide the means to exalt the Antichrist's beast over man. The prophecy of Revelation 13:11-18 states quite plainly that one day every man, woman and child will have to receive a universal code and number (666) and will have to worship the Antichrist as God or be killed.

As we see these things coming to pass, we wonder if this time is not nearer than most Christians dare to believe. The instructions of Paul to Christians as that day approaches is recorded in I Thessalonians 3:12-13:

> "And the Lord make you to increase and abound in love one toward another, and toward all men, even as we do toward you: To the end he may establish your hearts unblamable in holiness before God, even our Father, at the coming of our Lord Jesus Christ with all his saints."

7
COMPUTER OVER PEOPLE

The books of Daniel and Revelation clearly project that a day will come on the earth when a world dictator will command everyone to worship him as God. This evil personality will give a mark and a number to everyone in every nation, and he will have the power of life and death at his command. That this day is coming is a certainty. The Bible declares it, and we believe it.

In our previous study on *Computer Over Beast* we presented documented evidence that animal identification and control is making progress through the implementation of a code-numbering system whereby the subject might be identified by translating the mark into a six-digit number. Such a code mark and numbering system has been suggested for people. If it will work for animals, it will certainly work for human beings.

Also, in experiments using wild animals, electric transponders have been increasingly used to track animals. These too have been suggested for use in people control. The January 1975 edition of

COMPUTER OVER PEOPLE

Psychology Today, in an article titled, "The Electronic Watchdog We Shouldn't Use," reported:

> "Recently government and industry have poured money into research on mass transit hoping to replace dirty autos with clean monorails ... engineers have spent a lot of green developing gadgets to monitor the location of individual buses or trains in complex transportation networks. According to Harvard lawyer and lecturer in psychology, Ralph Schwitzgebel, the same instruments modified only slightly, can monitor people ... to prove his idea is feasible, and to study its psychological and social effects, Schwitzgebel and his colleagues constructed a crude prototype of an electronic watchdog system. They outfitted 16 volunteers with transceivers, set up receiving stations, and monitored their subjects' whereabouts.
>
> "One participant was a businessman, another a student, a third a mental patient. Several were prisoners who offered to join the project as an alternative to being locked up ... Seven individuals quit after five days, four more dropped out after 10 days. But three people continued to be monitored for more than a month, and one soul stuck with the researchers for over five months. 'Most of the subjects didn't adapt to the system,' says Schwitzgebel, 'but a few did.' He believes with a few incentives of legal constraints, most people could adjust. And with a little more sophisticated equipment,

> *the researchers say they could communicate with their subjects through tone signals. One tone could ask the patient to call the monitor, others could reward him for being where he should or warn him for being where he shouldn't.*
>
> *"Schwitzgebel no longer is testing or developing monitoring equipment, however, because his first study proved we have the technology to monitor people if we want to. Schwitzgebel doesn't want to. 'At the present time I'm not in favor of using this equipment because I think it would be misused,' he says."*

A related article on the same computer program to use transponders to control people was written for *Ramparts* magazine in 1971:

> *"The latest weird idea to come from the Pentagon's Peacefare program is a scheme for attaching miniature electronic devices to criminals or other suspect citizens and keeping track of them by computer ... The Crime Deterrent Transponder System was developed by Joseph Meyer, a computer specialist who works at the National Security Agency ... The details of the plan were described by Meyer in the January 1971 issue of* Transaction on Aerospace and Electronic Systems, *a publication of the Institute of electrical and Electronics Engineers. Initially, the transponders would be attached to 20 million 'subscribers' as a condition of bail or parole. Each subscriber*

would be identified by a unique code, which would be transmitted several times a minute to a computer ... The computer would record the subscriber's location and compare it with a stored file that would 'specify the normal schedule for the subscriber (and) any territorial or curfew restrictions.' If the computer found the subscriber to be in violation of these restrictions, it would instruct the transponder to warn its wearer of the transgression. The transponders would be 'attached' in such a way that they could not be removed without the computer knowing it. Subscribers who discard or tamper with their transponders would be classified as 'renegades' and would be charged with a felony ... Meyer urges that 'the assignment should be done on a fairly long-term basis, so that the criminal will acquire long experience in not committing crimes.' In practice, the computer would effectively control the lives of the persons plugged into it. According to Meyer, 'the aim of the transponder surveillance scheme is to constrain criminals and arrestees into behaving like law-abiding citizens. If this aim is fulfilled, then most of the subscribers will do ordinary things like get up in the morning and go to work. At night they will stay close to home, to avoid being implicated in crimes. At their place of work, a human surveillance system will operate. Low-powered transceivers in their domiciles can monitor them indoors.' Meyer has a social theory to go along with his electronics plan: 'In a success-oriented society the manifestations of success are largely material-affluence. Yet not everyone attains the upper-income brackets. The noncriminal undergoes a long apprenticeship amid family and peer group to learn the motivations and skills necessary to get along in the society and thus seek affluence by conventional means. Most people attain a rather median level of affluence, and only at the cost of conformity and indebtedness. Part of the social conditioning is to enable people to accept this limited success, and to feel guilty about it, without trying to upset the social and economic house of cards ... A transponder surveillance system can surround the criminal with a kind of externalized conscience — an electronic substitute for the social conditioning, group pressures, and inner motivation which most of the society lives with ... many criminals and miscreants seem to have little desire to go along with the social norms, so an externalized control system may be necessary to them, like a heart pacer to a cardiac patient.'"

From available evidence that we have, we know the following things about the computerized transponder control system:
1. For years radio transponders have been used to track and monitor the activity of animals, birds, and fish.
2. The system was employed in an experiment on 16 persons.

3. The transponder can be tied to a preprogrammed computer with a specific program for each individual, or the same program used for a particular class of individuals.

4. The computer can tell the persons to whom the unit is attached when to go to bed, when to go to work, when to go to the store, etc.

5. The initial proposal was to use the computerized control system co-jointly with a code-mark system on 20 million people for penal reasons. However, it would be technically feasible to institute such a people control program on a world-wide basis. By using satellites, it would be possible to control every person in every nation by giant preprogrammed computers.

Once again, the books of Daniel and Revelation project that in a coming world dictatorship, one man will be able to control the earth's population and demand that everyone worship him as God. Every person will be required to have his own mark and number or else they will not be able to work, buy or sell. Quoting Revelation 13:16, 17:

> *"And he causeth all, both small and great, rich and poor, free and bond, to receive a mark in their right hand, or in their foreheads: And that no man might buy or sell, save he that had the mark, or the name of the beast, or the number of his name."*

It is difficult to realize that there is now the technical knowledge and hardware to do it. In an article titled "The Computer Society" that appeared in the February 20, 1978, edition of *Time,* there is a subtitle, "The Age of Miracle Chips — New Microtechnology Will Transform Society":

> *"It is tiny, about a quarter of an inch square, and quite flat. Under a microscope, it resembles a stylized Navaho rug or the aerial view of a railroad switching yard. Like the grains of sand on a beach, it is made mostly of silicon, next to oxygen the most abundant element on the surface of the earth. Yet this inert fleck — still unfamiliar to the vast majority of Americans — has astonishing powers that are already transforming society. For the so-called miracle chip has a calculating capability equal to that of a room-size computer of only 25 years ago. Unlike the hulking Calibans of vacuum tubes and tangled wires from which it evolved, it is cheap, easy to mass produce, fast, infinitely versatile and convenient. Those outside the electronic priesthood often have trouble grasping the principles of the new microtechnology or comprehending the accomplishments of the minuscule computers ... The rapid proliferation of microcomputers will doubtless cause many social dislocations ... All of the prodigies of technology leave many people not only nostalgic for simpler times but alarmed by the unknown dangers ... Practically any breakthrough in knowledge carries with it the possibility that it will be used for evil ... Says Isaac Asimov, the prolific author and futuristic polymath: 'We are reaching the stage where the problems that we must*

COMPUTER OVER PEOPLE

> *solve are going to become insoluble without computers. I do not fear computers. I fear the lack of them'... There seems little doubt that life in the U.S., then in the rest of the industrial world, and eventually all over the planet, will be incalculably changed by the new microtechnology."*

The same amount of work that was done by an average room-sized computer 25 years ago, can now be done by a tiny chip one-fourth of an inch square, or about the size of a black-eyed pea. It is not mere science fiction now to visualize a satellite computer with ground transponders controlling the day-to-day activities of people all over the North American continent. The article in *Time* brings out the fact that we have passed the computer point of no return, and it is no longer a fear of a computer-controlled society that haunts the business world, but rather a fear that the computer will be taken away, or that there will not be enough computer power to supervise the uncertain nuclear age and space age. This anxious uncertainty for scientists is like the answer I gave someone not long ago when asked if I had a fear of flying. I replied, "No, I do not have a fear of flying, just a fear of falling."

That the federal government is ever tightening the control on individuals is beyond question. We quote from an article, dateline Washington, that appeared in the August 11, 1980 edition of *Army Times:*

> *"Military people, retirees and dependents of both are expected to receive new plastic identification cards similar to*

credit cards after October 1981. After completion of a six-month test at the Armed Forces Staff College, the new cards have been approved by the Defense Department and money for them has been budgeted for February 1982. The new cards are slated initially to replace both ID's and the medical privilege cards now used by dependents. Later, the cards could replace meal cards and other types of local identification. They will be tied into a worldwide computer system that is expected to cut fraud and misuse of ID's according to Pentagon officials ... When the cards are fed into an electronic card reader, medical offices will be able to tell within seconds if a person's card is valid and for what benefits the holder is authorized ... It will spread to the central Pacific Coast during August and to the rest of the United States by 1982. It will become worldwide in 1983."

The new identification card has become a badge with a transponder or preprogrammed microchip in it. The identification process is secured by the computer. One day, such a system will require a super-computer that will dispense food, medical services, and all kinds of commodities to those who have the proper identification mark or number (Rev. 13:16, 17).

To demonstrate how the mark is even now being made ready, I quote *Prophecy in the News*, November 1985, by J. R. Church, page 1, entitled: Mark of the Beast Tested in Sweden:

COMPUTER OVER PEOPLE

> "Believe it or not, some 6,000 people in Sweden have agreed to accept a mark on their right hand in order to test a new method of money exchange — in preparation for a future totally cashless society — says the Journal of the Australian Banks Employees Union."

The report was published recently by Peter LaLonde, editor of *The Prophecy Newsletter.* He said that confirmation had been extremely difficult, but quoted another source, *Ministries Behind the Iron Curtain Newsletter,* which published the following firsthand report:

> "While in Sweden I made a special effort to find more facts about the matter. At certain banks they had no or little knowledge about it, and seemed to brush it off.
>
> "However, I got a lead to the Executive Director's office in Stockholm, and made a special appointment with them.
>
> "There I was told that it is a fact, and the mark was done on the hand, and it was in the southeastern area of Sweden. They also told me the same experiment had been done in Japan and the Republic of Dominique in Latin America. Their remark was that the general public was not quite ready for it, but that perhaps In two years the government could pass a law making the practice mandatory.
>
> "It is important for Christians to note that the general public would be against the mark of the beast and, therefore, must be

psychologically prepared for this future event.

"Articles are beginning to appear which condemn Christians as lunatics for opposing electric funds transfers.

"A recent article in a Toronto newspaper described an additional lunacy which has entered the discussion.

"There are certain groups who feel that the evolution of the banking system is the devil's work — the development of coding schemes to mark merchandise and the possibility of electronic payment mechanisms will lead to each individual being coded with the mark of the beast which will become an integral part of every business transaction.

"Very few people will place any credence in that hysterical approach.

"It should come as no surprise that the Bible prophecy of a future mark of the beast will increasingly become the focus of such attacks as the day draws near."

But in spite of the perilous times in which we live, the world has hope. It is called "The Blessed Hope" in the Bible. Paul wrote to Titus that Christians should be "denying ungodliness and worldly lusts, we should live soberly, righteously, and godly, in this present world; Looking for that blessed hope and the glorious appearing of the great God and our Savior Jesus Christ" (Titus 2:12-13).

Jesus Christ is called the "Blessed Hope" within the context of Scripture relating to the last days; because without Him, we would be without hope. He is the hope of the world today because we read in Revelation 11:18 that He is coming back to save the earth from those who would destroy it.

8
An E.F.T. or an S.D.R

EFT means Electronic Funds Transfer. This is a computerized system of banking whereby funds are transferred by means of an electronic entry from one account to another without the benefit of cash or checks.

The service of money exchange in its various forms, which we generally refer to as banking, first began in ancient Babylon about 600 B.C. Banking was as much a part of the overall Babylonian system as the forced worship of the king as a god. It was more convenient and much safer to issue a merchant a note for gold and silver, and then when the bearer arrived at his destination, a banking associate would redeem the note for the same amount in precious metal. Of course a fee would be charged for the service. From this simple beginning, banking was extended to provide further services, including money lending and money exchange systems on both national and international levels. Today, there is the Federal Reserve, and also the World Bank and the International Monetary Fund.

The Word of God condemns the lending of money at exorbitant interest rates. According to Exodus 22:25, the poor were not to be charged any interest. It was acceptable to charge a fair rate of interest for business reasons, but the Bible warns that bankers can take over the control of the financial resources of the world.

It is obvious that if the banking industry continues to loan money at excessive interest rates, it will be only a matter of time before the banking establishment owns everything. The banking industry of nations, often at the instigation of politicians and rulers, have printed money out of paper and then charged interest on nothing. William Peterson, head of The Bank of England, said in 1694: "The bank hath benefit of interest on all moneys which it creates out of nothing."

Dr. Carroll Quigley, professor of history at Georgetown University, has written an extensive work on the history of world banking. The thrust of Dr. Quigley's investigation is that during the past 200 years, the banking families of the world have understood that in a time of expanded business and commerce on an international level, they have finally been given the golden opportunity sought since the time of Babylon. Dr. Quigley believes that world bankers can now bring all nations, regardless of political competition, under their control.

None of this is said to discredit or impugn local banks and bankers, which render an invaluable service. But the power of banking, like all other entities which daily touch the lives of people all over the world, can be misused for ungodly and tyrannical purposes.

Concerning the prophetic aspect of the financial structure of the world in the end of the age, and the part that the economic condition of the world will play in bringing to the forefront a world dictator, we know that the value of gold and silver will be decimated. We read in James 5:1-3:

> "Go to now, ye rich men, weep and howl for your miseries that shall come upon you. Your riches are corrupted, and your garments are moth-eaten. Your gold and silver is cankered; and the rust of them shall be a witness against you, and shall eat your flesh as it were fire. Ye have heaped treasure together for the last days."

Then we read of the time when the gold and silver will become worthless in verse 8, " ... the coming of the Lord draweth nigh." It is evident that James forecast a decline in the value of gold and silver to worthlessness as far as monetary value is concerned.

At a meeting of the international Monetary Fund in 1943, it was proposed that the gold reserve of the United States be taken from Ft. Knox and through various plans, including foreign aid, be distributed to other nations. The gold backed the paper U.S. dollars on foreign exchanges, thus giving the world a stable currency. During the next 20 years, U. S. paper money printed by the Federal Reserve flooded foreign nations through travel, foreign-based U.S. forces, commerce, foreign aid, and loans. United States' short-term notes were redeemable in gold from Ft. Knox at the ridiculously low rate of $42 an ounce. Foreign investors sold our $42 gold for $200

AN E.F.T. OR AN S.D.R.

an ounce. Soon, Ft. Knox was practically empty, and in 1963 President John F. Kennedy stood before the International Monetary Fund and boasted in reference to IMF's plan to give away gold, "It did not come about by chance, but by conscious and deliberate planning." Based on current gold prices, the United States taxpayers were literally robbed by the one-world economists of over $2 trillion, or about $7,000 for every man, woman and child in our nation.

The result is an unstable international monetary unit for trade and commerce.

World inflation was preplanned and preprogrammed by international one-worlders to bring to pass a world economic order over which a world dictatorship will reign. Whether the planners envisioned a UN dictatorship, a Communist dictatorship, or a trilateral dictatorship is a moot point. To paraphrase Shakespeare, "a world dictatorship by any other names is just as oppressive." The fact that world inflation was preordained by international masterminds was clearly brought out by Kevin Phillips, editorial writer for King Features Syndicate, in a March 24, 1977 article titled "New Economic Order Looms" in the *Oklahoma City Times:*

> *"Ten miles from downtown Washington, out on the rolling horse country of Potomac, MD, lies 'Bretton Woods,' the private country club operated by the International Monetary Fund and the World Bank ... Henry Hazlitt, the noted conservative economist, argues that in the 1945 Bretton Woods agreement setting up the IMF, foreign countries were in effect allowed to 'expand (print) money and credit more freely. If they got into trouble,*

> they had access to automatic borrowing rights from the new International Monetary Fund. The whole arrangement made it much safer to inflate.' According to Barron's, the national business weekly, easy loan mechanisms made the IMF 'an engine of global inflation.'"

It is noted in Revelation 6:5-6 concerning the part inflation will have in bringing in the Antichrist during the Great Tribulation:

> "And when he had opened the third seal, I heard the third beast say, Come and see. And I beheld, and lo a black horse; and he that sat on him had a pair of balances in his hand. And I heard a voice in the midst of the four beasts say, A measure of wheat for a penny, and three measures of barley for a penny; and see thou hurt not the oil and the wine."

Applying the value of a penny in the day this prophecy was given to the coming world inflation, it will require a day's wages to buy a loaf of bread. The fact that we are going to have a new money system is not the question; the question is how soon? Willard Cantelon observed in his book *The Day The Dollar Dies*:

> "In 1944 a World Bank was born, an infant that soon grew into a mighty giant ... with the formation of the IMF, other names began to appear prominently in the world arena, names such as the World Bank, the

AN E.F.T. OR AN S.D.R.

> *G-10 and the Gold Pool. It was a spokesman from the latter, on March 31, 1968, who introduced 'paper gold' ... It was neither paper nor gold but only a number placed by the name of the nation. The amount of that number was called 'drawing right' and was abbreviated with three initials 'SDR' standing for 'Special Drawing Rights.'"*

Consider the role of the Federal Reserve Board, the 12 Federal Reserve banks throughout the nation and their role in deflating or inflating money or even creating money out of thin air. Quoting Phoebe Courtney's *Tax Pamphlet,* Number 207, July 1985, page 6, entitled, "The Big Banks' Plan to Control Your Money":

> *"In a speech prepared by Washington State Senator Jack Metcalf for presentation at the National Conference of State Legislatures on December 10, 1982, Senator Metcalf stated that the Fed is a federally chartered, private banking consortium. It is empowered to act with absolutely no control by any elected person or body. Though the President appoints members of the Federal Reserve Board and they are confirmed by the Senate, they represent the banking community, and once in office, are completely beyond the reach of the public whose lives and businesses are deeply affected by their decisions. Neither their meetings nor the minutes of their meetings are open to the public. Further,*

> *there has never been an independent audit of the Fed. ... "*

The private ownership and control of the Federal Reserve System has been judicially recognized by the 9th Circuit Court of Appeals in Lewis vs. United States, 680 F 2d 1239, 1241 (9th Cir. 1982) where the court stated:

> *"Examining the organization and function of the Federal Reserve Banks, and applying the relevant factors, we conclude that the Reserve Banks are not federal instrumentalities for purposes of the FTCA (Federal Tort Claims Act), but are independent, privately owned and locally controlled corporations."*

Who owns the Fed?

Alan Stang, in the April 1985, issue of *American Opinion* Magazine furnished the following information:

> *"Who owns the Fed? The answer will tell us who controls the country. The Federal Reserve Bank of New York issued 203,053 shares. On May 19, 1914, the Bank told the comptroller of the Currency that the big New York banks had taken more than half of them. The Rockefeller National City Bank took the largest number of shares: 30,000. Morgan's First National Bank took 15,000 shares. When these two banks merged in 1955, they owned almost a quarter of the shares of the New York Fed, which controls*

AN E.F.T. OR AN S.D.R.

the system. The Chase National Bank, also a Rockefeller entity took 6,000 shares ...

"As of July 26, 1983, the official Rockefeller banks (Chase Manhattan and CitiBank) held almost 30 percent of the shares of the New York Fed."

Paul A. Volcker, was appointed Chairman of the Federal Reserve Board by President Jimmy Carter in 1979, and was reappointed by President Reagan.

Volcker had been president of the New York Federal Reserve Bank, and has held management positions at David Rockefeller's Chase Manhattan Bank, is a trustee of the Rockefeller Foundation, and a board member of Rockefeller's Council on Foreign Relations (CFR).

The Monetary Control Act of 1980:

At the instigation of the big banks, Congress passed and President Carter signed on March 31, 1980, the Depository Institutions Deregulation and Monetary Control Act, Public Law 96-221. This new law greatly increased the power of the Federal Reserve, yet few members of the Congress were aware of its dangerous implications. Under the new law the Fed can monetize (turn into new money) all sorts of debt instruments, including debts of foreign governments. The Fed can also buy up the debt of foreign banks if that debt is guaranteed by a foreign government. Using this foreign debt, as collateral, the Federal Reserve can issue more Federal Reserve Notes.

How this helps bail out the big banks is obvious: If, for example, Brazil or Romania can't pay their principal and interest when due to the New York banks, the Fed can literally print money or grant credit — using that foreign debt as security — then re-route the money to the lending banks to make current interest and principal payments. In fact, according to Congressman Ron Paul in a statement on March 23, 1983, the Fed has used foreign debt as collateral for issuing Federal Reserve Notes on at least 139 occasions, from April 1981 to January 1983 ...

In early May 1985, William M. Isaac, chairman of the Federal Deposit Insurance Corp (FDIC), told Congress that in 1984 the worst year for the banking industry since the Depression era. As of May 31, 1985, there had been 43 bank failures, so the total 1985 figure is expected to top 1984's total of 79.

Isaac also told Congress "that the number of problem banks is at an all-time high of 949."

The day is at hand when EFTs and SDRs will become the world's money unit. Special Drawing Rights will be granted to the individual by a world system, and these rights to work, buy, and sell with codes and marks that electronically transfer computer money units will be the future economic system.

What these signs mean is that the Word of God is sure. These are days to heed the advice of James, the brother of Jesus:

> *"Be patient therefore, brethren, unto the coming of the Lord. Behold, the husbandman waiteth for the precious fruit of the earth, and hath long patience for it, until he receive the early and latter rain. Be ye also patient; establish your hearts: for the coming of the Lord draweth nigh"* (James 5:7-8).

9
GAMBLING WITH CREDIT CARDS

In this division of our study on how the world is headed toward a cashless computerized economic order where everyone works, buys and sells using marks and numbers, we will be reviewing the part the modern credit card is playing in bringing this all about.

We can conclude that the trend toward universal credit and numbering people began in earnest with the Social Security numbering system. When Social Security and the NRA were first introduced in the early 1930's, there was much opposition from many churches. It was thought by many Christians that this was the beginning of the process by which everyone would be brought to worship the Antichrist as prophesied in Revelation 13.

The NRA program, with its self-identification symbol, was dropped because of the opposition, and then the nation was assured that the Social Security number would never be used for identification purposes outside the Social Security program. Of course we know that promise was never kept, because today an adult cannot get a job, a driver's license, cash a check, or obtain credit without a Social Security number. Without it, in today's world, a person is a non-entity.

With the coming of the computer age, numbers became of greater importance. Banking establishments and enterprising investors found that by using computers and numbering systems, credit card business could be a very lucrative one. The customer could be issued a plastic card, also known as plastic money, that would be honored at most places dispensing merchandise. It could also be used for travel, food and lodging. The amount charged would be guaranteed by the credit card company, which would in turn bill the customer. Large credit card companies like VISA, MasterCard, American Express, Diners, etc., have sprung up. Many oil companies and large department stores, or merchandising companies like Sears and Montgomery Ward, established their own credit cards. It has been reported that as much money is made in profit from credit cards as there is in the sale of merchandise.

But the credit card system has not been all good. This was brought out in the January 14, 1980 edition of *Fortune* magazine in an article entitled "Saving the Consumer from the Computerized Snafu." Even the Federal Reserve System was thwarted by a computer error. Quoting just a portion of this article:

> *"Millions of Americans could feel a wry sense of kinship with the Federal Reserve Board when Manufacturers Hanover, the fourth-largest commercial bank in the U.S., confessed in October that it had*

inadvertently loused up the nation's money-supply figures. Billions of dollars in errors over a three-week period, it will be recalled, led to a false impression that the money supply was expanding far more than was actually the case."

The article continues to cite cases in the credit card files that cause trouble for the seller and the buyer as well. Cases are cited involving Diners, MasterCard, VISA and others. We share one incident involving Allstate Insurance:

"The intertwining of human error and systems error was brilliantly encapsulated in a baffling experience that befell an Allstate policyholder. He had moved from Long Island to New York City ... Though he had sent a change of address, his new policy arrived at his old address. It was forwarded, and when he paid the $602 premium, he changed the address for a second time. Before long he began to wonder if he and Allstate were still on the same planet. Rates in New York City are higher than in the suburbs, and the computer generated a new bill for an additional $207.80. The customer thought this was much too high, since one of his cars was still garaged on Long Island. He did not pay the bill, but on May 23 complained by letter. The agent agreed with him, but Allstate headquarters showed no such understanding. During the summer, the policyholder was surprised to receive both a

credit of $103.90 and another bill for $258, which he did not pay. The computer gradually became more insistent in the bills it ground out. The customer again complained to his agent, who finally advised him to make a payment, lest his policy be cancelled. He remitted $150 in August. Then, with no more explanation than in the past, in September he received a refund of $238.40 — then an additional refund in December, of $23.70. The first refund had been incorrectly calculated. Embarrassed officials agreed to investigate. It was a tangled tale."

An increasingly serious problem that has developed within the credit card business itself is inflation and rising interest rates. We quote from "Now It's the No-Credit Card," in the September 29, 1980 edition of *Time*.

"It looks and feels like a credit card, and it can ring up purchases as easily. But Master Card II, which was introduced last week, is not the same as familiar plastic money. With the normal credit card, the bill for a shopping spree may not arrive for weeks. But with Master Card II, which bankers call a debit card, payment takes place instantly. A computer deducts funds from the shopper's bank account and transfers them into that of the store or restaurant where purchases have been made. Cardholders may carry either the regular MasterCard, Master Card II, or both

> ... MasterCard will have to struggle. Five years ago, VISA introduced the first debit card ... Yet both cards face serious troubles. In the past, most profits have come from consumers who only paid interest on their bills rather than settling them in full each month. But when interest rates soared last spring, banks lost money on their card business. Indeed, Jack Cox, publisher of a newsletter about bank cards, estimates that U.S. banks lost at least $250 million on credit card operations in the first half of March ... MasterCard use fell 8.4 percent during the first quarter of the year, and from March to July, Americans decreased their consumer debt by about $6 million. VISA and MasterCard users will now have to pay more for using plastic."

Because of the problems arising in the credit card market, a new no-money scheme concerning a credit card-check arrangement is evolving. We quote from an ad headlined "NCNB's Checkmate ... The 'Plastic Check' ":

> "You're shopping where you're not known. You see something you want to buy and you want to pay by check ... but the shopkeeper looks at you doubtfully. He's taken a few bad checks in his time, and he wants you to dig down deep for your driver's license, a credit card ... he may even demand your fingerprints! After a lot of hesitation, he may accept your check. Or maybe he turns it down. It's inconvenient.

But now NCNB has eliminated this problem with CHECKMATE ... The Plastic Check ... Instead of writing a check, you present CHECKMATE. It looks like a VISA card ... except that the words NCNB CHECKMATE appear in the blue band at the top of the card ... and anyone who accepts VISA will accept CHECKMATE. That includes over 2 1/2 million establishments ... in your neighborhood, across the U.S. and around the world ... But a Checkmate transaction is not a credit transaction. The amount you've spent for your purchase is deducted directly from your NCNB checking account, just as if you've written a check ... By creating your own personal identification code, you can also use your CHECKMATE card in our NCNB 24 Banking Machines to find out your checking balance, or get cash, or make a deposit to your checking or savings account ... or to transfer funds from your savings to your checking account — or vice versa. Your own personal identification code should be composed of any combination of six numbers or letters ... be sure to enter your code in the space provided on the certificate of the enclosed letter.'

As we have already noted, credit card business is becoming passé. Plans for immediate EFT money using nothing but code marks and numbers is coming into being. Each person with his or her own code mark or number can do business around the world, controlled from a central location. We noted with interest that the plan just referred to calls for a

GAMBLING WITH CREDIT CARDS 111

six-digit number for everyone in this particular computer funds transfer company. We read again of the coming economic program of Antichrist in Revelation 13:16-18:

> "And he causeth all, both small and great, rich and poor, free and bond, to receive a mark in their right hand, or in their foreheads: And that no man might buy or sell, save he that had the mark, or the name of the beast, or the number of his name. Here is wisdom. Let him that hath understanding count the number of the beast: for it is the number of man; and his number is six hundred threescore and six."

Another step in the direction of the Antichrist system appeared in the March 2, 1979 edition of *The Detroit News,* in an article titled "An Electronic Flash May be Future Cash":

> "It will cost you to pay cash in the so-called 'cashless society' of the year 2000 simply because coins and bills are harder to handle than electronic impulses. Even the use of checks and credit cards will gradually decline in the turn-of-the-millennium's new money system. That system will consist of one national credit card; an innovation known as the debit card; and the ultimate in efficiency and impersonality — what the Swedes call the 'Person Number' ... (In the U.S. it could well be your Social Security number).

"You present your personal number when you buy something. The cashier taps out the number on the computer keyboard, and instantly one of three lights come on. Green says you have funds in your banks to cover the cost of the purchase. Amber says you're temporarily overdrawn, but that you have a history of making a fresh deposit in time to meet your obligations. The message to the cashier: Sell at your own risk. Red says just what you think it does. The electronic transfer of funds on a mass scale sounds like too much too soon, but people who study such innovations insist it's technologically possible right now ... A complete electronic funds transfer system will start with authorizing your employer to electronically transmit your paycheck to the bank. The bank's computer will pay your mortgage installment, utilities, insurance premiums and make deposits in your checking and savings account. More elaborate packages could even include the computation of your income tax and the electronic transfer of your tax liability to the Internal Revenue Service ... With few people carrying cash, a decrease in robberies is likely. And fewer mailbox break-ins may result from fewer payments going through the mails ... To the disappointment of many people, instant electronic deductions from your bank account augurs an end to the celebrated American practice of 'kiting,' or 'floating,' checks. No longer will you be able to buy Friday's groceries on an

> *empty checkbook and rely on a Monday bank deposit being in early enough to keep you honest. And Cetron thinks the computers may force some businessmen to straighten up their books: you know, one set for themselves, one set for their partner, and one set for the IRS. But in this new society there ain't no way to play games."*

As we watch the modern computerized checkout stand reading code marks and numbers, and with introduction of the debit card with each individual's number or mark on it, all that is needed to fulfill the prophecy in Revelation 13 is to transfer the mark or number to the hand or forehead, where the computer screen reads directly off the individual instead of the card. When the national identity, or debit card, becomes mandatory, theft and fraud will be a problem. However, if the mark or number is on the person, then that problem would be resolved. That a national identity mark or number is coming is certain. We quote from the September 15, 1980 *U.S. News & World Report:*

> *"In this time of high unemployment, it is natural that demands again are growing for Washington to do something about illegal aliens — the multiplying legions sneaking into this country and taking jobs needed by citizens ... The big problem is that there is presently no sure way for an employer to tell whether a job applicant is 'legal' or 'illegal.' So a Select Commission on Immigration and Refugee Policy, created by Congress, is now seeking ways to solve this problem.*

Several methods are being studied. One would create a new employee identification card that could be obtained only with documented proof of eligibility and would be hard to counterfeit. Any person seeking a job would be required to show the card. Another idea under consideration is to use the Social Security card as a means of identification. To do this, however, the Social Security card would have to be made much more secure against trickery. The present card is not very difficult to obtain and is easy to counterfeit. Thousands, possibly millions, of fake cards are now in use ... The idea of using Social Security cards runs into many objections. One critic is Patricia Harris, Secretary of Health and Human Services, whose department administers the Social Security system. She estimates it would cost about $850 million and take at least five years to issue 'tamper resistant' cards to all new applicants and replace the cards now in use ... 'Also there could be substantial adverse reaction from the public ... ' She stresses that 'our society has had a long history of opposition to the concept of a universal identifier, and I share this concern' ... However, it is increasingly clear that something has to be done ... False IDs are used not only to get jobs but for many kinds of fraud including relief frauds, that costs this country and its businesses many millions of dollars ... Ironically: Mexico, a major source of this country's illegal aliens, is now having an 'illegal' problem of its own from an

> *invasion of people fleeing Central America. So Mexico's president recently ordered the very step that the U.S. has been reluctant to take — issuance of a national identity card to all his country's residents, Mexican or foreign."*

Thus, we see the numbering of people in the Social Security System has gradually developed into a national, even a projected, worldwide numbering system. In gambling with a credit card system of buy now and pay later, the American people, and possibly all the world, have ushered in the debit card. The underlying concern regarding all such identification, numbering, and cashless society plans, is the loss of identity cards, marks and numbers. The next logical step is to imprint a person's number by laser beam on the hand or on the forehead. The economic world of the Antichrist, in which all the world will have to worship this false messiah as God, or have their number or mark taken away, is now very possible. The coming of the Lord is very near, even at the door.

10
THE ULTIMATE COMPUTER

In this chapter we will be considering the "ultimate computer."

Almost every month new discoveries in the computer field make the computers of a year ago obsolete.

But the ultimate in future computers may well be described in Revelation 13:13-15:

> "And he doeth great wonders, so that he maketh fire come down from heaven on the earth in the sight of men. And deceiveth them that dwell on the earth by the means of those miracles which he had power to do in the sight of the beast; saying to them that dwell on the earth, that they should make an image to the beast which has the wound by a sword, and did live. And he had power to give life unto the image of the beast, that the image of the beast should both speak, and cause that as many as would not worship the image of the beast should be killed."

THE ULTIMATE COMPUTER

The description provided by the apostle John of this monstrosity is an image, or a machine. If it talks and controls the economy of the world through marks and numbers it would of necessity have to be machine-like. More and more the image of Antichrist appears to be the final product of modern computer science.

The image-making computer is already in the offing. The March 12, 1979 edition of *Aviation Week & Space Technology* on page 181 states:

> *"Image Systems Developed: General Electric Co., with a firm commitment to computer-generated imagery systems, is pursuing the high-technology end of the business, developing a full-daylight, computer-generated imagery system ... with in-line infinity optics."*

Thus, the image of the beast described in Revelation 13 becomes more real with each passing day: an ultimate computer with infinite optical and memory capabilities. This means that action is immediate rather than depending upon stored information or retarded readout reaction. This development is another step forward in the creation of an ultimate computer.

In addition to taking over the supervision of the social and economic worlds, computers are now intruding into the domestic spheres of everyday life. Computers that turn on television sets, coffee pots, and regulate other household appliances are becoming common. Computers are now made to do the family bookkeeping and pay the monthly household bills. Computers are replacing security guards and watchdogs, because they are less expensive and better. According to the August 8, 1979 edition of the *Seattle Post-Intelligencer,* a super-sleuth Honeywell Delta 1000 Computer caught 21 burglars in the Seattle schools in just one month. To illustrate the almost human development of the computer, we quote from a few headlines of articles that appeared in recent years:

TALKING COMPUTER: A headline in the July 28, 1980 edition of *Business Week* reads, "Talking chips: Now, more choices." Computers can not only talk in English, they can be programmed to talk in many languages. An ad in the May 1980 edition of *Omni* reads, "I only speak English, but, with my Craig translator, I can make myself understood to over 2 billion people."

AUTOMOBILE: Computers are being installed in cars. The October 1980 edition of the magazine *Discover* announces "Detroit's Brainy" will be installed with a computer to make your automobile get "Better gas mileage, give off far less pollution, and provide a remarkable variety of convenient, useful and amusing devices to make driving safer, less expensive, and more fun."

THE ARTS: Also in the October 1980 edition of *Discover* is a six-page story on computer artists. Computers are being programmed to take over much of the artwork for merchandise designs and newspaper advertising.

TELEVISION-TELEPHONE: An ad in the October 1980 edition of *Scientific American* reads, "Hubie answers the television. Zenith announces Space Phone. It's amazing! Now you can answer the telephone right through your new Zenith System."

THE ULTIMATE COMPUTER

TWO-WAY TELEVISION: A recent ad in the magazine *Technology* announced, "2-Way TV Is Here!" It reads, "Crosswits host Jack Clark ... pits the contestants in the studio against viewers at home ... The entire scene builds to a frenzy as studio and home contestants vie for the most points and big prizes."

Also, computers are on the drawing board with the ability of facial recognition. It will obey, or respond, only to its master. But the 13th chapter of Revelation projects a machine with a personality, an image or an object that everyone will be commanded to worship, and we read that most of the world at that time will willingly do so. Movies like *Star Wars* have already given man-like computers personality. Why will hundreds of millions of people worship an inanimate object that possibly will be a supercomputer? I quote from an article entitled "The Computer Backlash," from page 1 of the August 2, 1979 edition of *The Chicago Tribune:*

> *"To computer scientists who understood it, the ELIZA program was a sort of high-level doodling, a mechanical trick that told the researchers something about a computer's ability to utilize English grammar. But to nonexperts who used it, the computer program became much more. Developed at the Massachusetts Institute of Technology in 1966, the ELIZA program mimicked a psychotherapist interviewing a patient. It was named for the character in George Bernard Shaw's 'Pygmalion' who learned to speak upper-class English. ELIZA'S instructions enabled the computer*

to recognize certain words and formulate English-sentence responses ... An example of the dialogue:

Person: I'm unhappy.

Computer: Do you think coming here will help you not to be unhappy?

Person: I need some help, that much seems certain.

Computer: What would it mean to you if you got some help?

Person: Perhaps I could learn to get along with my mother.

Computer: Tell me more about your family.

" ... to the horror of Joseph Weizenbaum, the MIT professor who wrote the program, the patients began to develop 'relationships' with ELIZA. They confided in the computer, waited to be alone with it, attributed empathy to it. It was not long before doctors and other computer scientists were calling Weizenbaum and suggesting that 'computer psychotherapists' be put beside couches. The realization that computers could have such a powerful influence on people — and that computer experts were ready to apply these powerful tools with such 'recklessness' changed Weizenbaum's whole outlook on the field. He went from being one of the nations's most-respected computer researchers to being one of the field's most outspoken critics."

THE ULTIMATE COMPUTER 121

The Bible apparently is somehow linked to the computer. We believe God has His own computerized system in His divine administration of the Universe. Whereby every spoken and or written word of all history is recorded and nothing is lost.

Malachi 3:16: "Then they that feared the Lord spake often one to another: and the Lord hearkened, and heard it, and a book of remembrance was written before him for them that feared the Lord, and that thought upon his name."

It seems that man's computer is also unlocking some of the hidden things of God in His Word.

As we did in this book's introduction, we quote — in part — a November 26, 1985, *Houston Chronicle* article entitled "VOICE BEHIND THE WORD — Computer Used to Trace Bible's 'Divine Source'."

> *"JERUSALEM (UPI) — Israeli researchers using a computer say they have found encoded messages in the Bible giving support to the belief that the book's every word is divinely inspired ...*
>
> *" 'There is no way to explain this information,' said Dr. Moshe Katz, a Technion biomechanic who has a degree in biblical studies. '*
>
> *"Katz said he and Dr. Fred Weiner, a computer specialist on the Technion medical faculty, told the computer to skip letters as it scanned the Hebrew language Bible. Often words and messages leaped out of the text when the computer used only every 50th letter or 26th letter ...*
>
> *"The number '50,' Katz pointed out, is seven times seven plus one. Seven is an*

important number in the Bible. There are seven days in the week of creation. It is 50 days between Passover and Shavuot (Pentecost). Farmers were told to work the land 49 years and rest it on the 50th year.

"Katz said that by skipping letters, the computer found 'Elohim,' another Hebrew name for God, hidden 147 times among the letters of the book of Genesis. He said the probability of it happening by chance was about one in 2 million.

"Computer programmer Dr. Eliyahu Rips, a Hebrew University mathematician, found the name of Aaron, the high priest, hidden among the letters in the first part of Leviticus 25 times. He said the probability of that happening was one in 500,000.

"Esther 9 is the story of how Queen Esther demanded the hanging of the 10 sons of Haman, who were enemies of the Jews. Hidden among the names of the sons were letters of the Hebrew date for 1946 — the year the Nazis were hanged ...

"In Deuteronomy 31, the Lord told Moses his descendants would forsake God and break His law. Deuteronomy says, 'When my anger will be kindled against them ... and I will devour them.'

"When the computer read every 50th letter in that section, the Hebrew word for 'holocaust' emerged.

"Many biblical scholars today believe the Bible was pieced together by a skilled editor using four ancient sources — the 'D,' 'P,' 'E' and 'J' documents.

THE ULTIMATE COMPUTER

"There is no way that this documentary hypothesis can stand," Katz said. Under the team's theory, if even one letter is removed, all the results collapse.

"The project aroused mixed reactions. Chaim Gevaryahu, head of the Israel Bible Society, said the program was controversial, but the team members were 'serious people and people of science.'

" 'Why is it necessary for the Almighty to use numbers?' Gevaryahu said. 'I would like to say that in biblical scholarship, we don't use these methods.' "

Yet, all is not well for the Christian in Computerland. The computer of the future is a marriage counselor, a friend in need, a watchdog, financial adviser, a psychiatrist, and the perfect babysitter.

The Ultimate Computer envisioned by some is one that would control every business transaction in the world, regulate all national and international communications and traffic, and the daily behavior pattern of every individual. In other words, the daily life of every individual on this planet, including working, buying, and selling, would be controlled from a central source. This would bring the perfect harmony desired and eliminate all waste, conflicts, and harmful competition between individuals as well as organizations and governments.

Documentation: *Computerworld,* May 17, 1982, (page 19) —

"By the year 2000 people will be 'marrying' robots as surrogate human

beings ... suggested Arthur Harkins, director of the graduate program in future research here at the University of Minnesota. 'The great bulk of human relationships are formulated on a ritualistic basis, which is to say that most humans, in their relationships with wives or lovers, expect a kind of metronomic precision of expected behavior and expected responses to occur over a time,' Harkins said in a recent interview. ' ... when we do get A-1 in the late '90s or early 21st century ... we should be able to have humans paired off with machines in such a way that the comparison between their two capabilities (will) allow us, in some cases, to define them as equal ... It seems imminently possible to program software to meet those types of needs. When you add voice recognition, voice synthesis and at least limited mobility, you don't even need artificial intelligence ... The 'marriage' need not conform to the standard Christian approach of 'for a lifetime.' It may be for a weekend, for a day, for a year ... '
Supposing robots can be programmed with pleasing personalities or a temper, a sense of humor or a musical talent, will their companion-ability extend to sexual liaisons? Yes, according to Harkins. 'The Japanese have already developed all kinds of mechanical substitutes for human sexual organs, which are implanted in a robot and can be embellished with heat and other types of human-like characteristics,' he reported. In addition, it will become more

and more difficult to physically distinguish robots from humans ... 'The metal, fiber or carbon filament ... will be concealed by a decorative outer covering, which could be clothing, fur or an artificial skin with the warmth and texture of healthy human skin' ... What about marriage as the sacramental joining of two people 'in the eyes of God?' 'The theologians are basically unwilling to deal with any of this,' Harkins said."

Inasmuch as men and women are finding it increasingly difficult to experience fulfillment in each other, computerized robots are being designed that will be everything a man or woman may want. Order to exact specifications. The image of the beast that will speak and command everyone to take his mark and number could be the ultimate computer idol or god.

U.S. intelligence agencies depend on supercomputers to sort through the enormous quantities of surveillance data beamed home by ground-based listening posts and orbiting spy satellites. By using supercomputers to simulate explosion, nuclear weapons experts require fewer test explosions to validate their designs. Machines like the Cray-2 are essential to any Star Wars defensive system for locating and intercepting incoming missiles before they re-enter the atmosphere.

Computers of 20 years ago that filled rooms have now been reduced to the approximate size and shape of a man, and computer capability and memory is at least doubling every year. With computer imagery, vastly expanding memory systems and brains, it is possible within the foreseeable future to create a single computer the size of a man that could control the activities of every person in the world. All the world would look to this single supercomputer for answers to all problems.

Computers are already replacing factory workers, doctors, psychiatrists, psychologists, and school teachers. More and more the world is looking to the computer as an idol or a god of the world of finance, economics, and possibly even religion. We believe that the increase of knowledge and modern science has set the stage for the fulfillment of the prophecies of Revelation 13 in our lifetime.

11
THE MARK AND THE NUMBER

Of the economic system that will demand every person on planet Earth to reject Jesus Christ as Lord and Savior and worship a false messiah as their god we refer again to Revelation 13:16-18:

> *"And he causeth all, both small and great, rich and poor, free and bond, to receive a mark in their right hand, or in their foreheads: And that no man might buy or sell, save he that had the mark, or the name of the beast, or the number of his name. Here is wisdom. Let him that hath understanding count the number of the beast: for it is the number of a man; and his number is six hundred threescore and six."*

The mechanics of such a system, as we have brought out several times in this study, were not possible until the present generation. To demand that everyone in the world buy, work and sell by using code marks and numbers would require an accounting method that would have staggered the imagination before the advent of the computer. In a long list of the evolving uses of computers given in the July 19, 1976, edition of *U.S. News and World Report* one is of particular note:

> *"Helping doctors to determine which terminally ill patient should die and which should live." According to this article, computers are helping to determine which terminally ill patients in hospitals should be treated and which should be allowed to die. This is just one small step from the world of the Tribulation period when the image of the beast will determine who should live and who should die in all nations.*
>
> *"According to the revelation of the last days given to the apostle John, everyone will be required to have a mark, or a code mark, on their forehead, and/or a number in their hand. The code mark on the forehead could be the same as the number in their hand, because code marks are readily changed by a computer scanner to numbers that identify products, animals, or even people."*

An article in the August 8, 1975 *San Jose Mercury* titled "They Really Have Your Number" stated in part:

> *"By using three six-digital units, the entire world could be assigned a working number — an international mark that would do away with all currency and coin. Instead, credit notes could be exchanged through a*

world bank clearing center. No member could buy or sell without having a digital mark. One man could have at his fingertips the number of any man on earth."

We are actually very close today to the three six-digital units. An article in *The Daily Oklahoman,* October 30, 1980, entitled, "Get Ready For 9-Digit Zip Codes" reported:

"The U.S. Postal Service in its wisdom, apparently feeling we have too little on our minds, soon will require each of us to memorize a nine-digit zip code number in place of our present five-digit cipher."

Consider this: if we are to soon have a new nine-digit zip code, combine this with your nine-digit Social Security number, and what do you have? Eighteen numbers that will identify you around the world, or three sixes.

The number 666 is an interesting one, because six is the number of man. Man was created on the sixth day and God ordained that man should work six days out of seven. Because six is one short of seven, the perfect number, it brands man as an imperfect creature — never becoming perfect through his own works and knowledge apart from God. The number 666 identifies man as the enemy of God. Goliath was six cubits in height, and his spearhead weighed 600 shekels of iron.

Nebuchadnezzar, before the judgment of God came upon him for his pride, was a type of Antichrist. Like the coming Antichrist, Nebuchadnezzar built an image and commanded all the world to worship it or be killed. The image of this previous world dictator was 60 cubits high, six cubits broad, and the band which played the music for this religious abomination was composed of six different instruments. The Bible says that a day is coming when the number 666 stamped on people will label them as Satan's property.

The magazine *Senior Scholastics*, September 20, 1973, startled students of prophecy when an article titled "Public Needs and Private Right — Who is Watching You?" stated in part:

> *"All buying and selling in the program will be done by computer. No currency, no change, no checks. In the program, people would receive a number that had been assigned them tattooed in their wrist or forehead. The number is put on by a laser beam and cannot be felt. The number in the body is not seen with the naked eye and is as permanent as your fingerprints. All items of consumer goods will be marked with a computer mark. The computer outlet in the store which picks up the number on the items at the checkstand will also pick up the number in the person's body and automatically total the price and deduct the amount from the person's 'Special Drawing Rights' account ... "*

The First National Bank of Memphis uses an advertising logo with a number on a head under the slogan: "My Number's Right On The top of My Head — Only You and the Computer Know Your Number." *The Chicago Sun Times* has already reported that some people are having their Social Security number, or other identification numbers tattooed on their bodies. When the "Mark of the Beast" arrives, many may rush to be first in line to get their own personal code mark imprinted on their foreheads.

The November 1976 edition of *Reader's Digest* carries an interesting story related to our subject entitled "Coming Soon: Electronic Money":

> "George Johnson and millions of other senior citizens never see a Social Security check. Their pension payments are deposited into their bank accounts electronically, with no paper changing hands ...
>
> "Nearly one million American workers, including nearly the entire active duty U.S. Air Force, now have wages or salaries automatically deposited in their bank accounts by means of magnetic tape.
>
> "Half a million others make regular payments for rents, loans, bills, etc. in the same manner, without signing anything ... At the checkout counters of several hundred supermarkets in the United States, no cash or checks need change hands.
>
> "The clerk simply slips your plastic 'debit' card into an electronic terminal connected by telephone line to the bank's computer, and the cost of your groceries is instantly transferred from your bank account to the store's. Automatic Teller Machines are located in shopping centers, apartment complexes, airports, factories, hospitals, or the outside of banks. They will give you your

bank balance, issue you up to $100 a day from your account, accept cash and checks for deposit, transfer funds between savings, checking and credit accounts, and present you with a printed receipt for each transaction.

"In Minneapolis you may conduct financial transactions without ever leaving your home. By pushing the proper keys on your touch-tone telephone, you direct a computer in your savings bank to switch funds from your account to the accounts of stores, utilities, etc. ...

"On the back of each card is a magnetic stripe with your PIN number and/or bank account number micro-encoded ... If you make a mistake, the machine will tell you and wait for you to correct it ... After each withdrawal, the computer records your new balance, and it will not honor the next transaction made with the card if you are overdrawn or have exceeded a daily limit ...

"In this new, totally electronic age, the enforcement of financial obligations will present few difficulties, since failure to pay up could be disastrous.

"The culprit might even be forced to undergo what EFT men call 'plastic surgery' — the cutting off of his bank cards ... Economically speaking, this would make him a non-person."

The editors of *Reader's Digest* probably were totally unaware of how closely they were to reporting

THE MARK AND THE NUMBER

the fulfilling of Bible prophecy relating to the world of Antichrist.

The September 21, 1976 edition of *The Daily Oklahoman* reported:

> "The long-talked about 'cashless society' is almost here. Bank debit cards are expected to go into nationwide use soon, and the U.S. Mint has recommended abolition of half dollars and pennies ...
>
> "Payment of bills by debit card is coming. Computer coded prices on items at supermarkets will make it possible for customers to obtain groceries without seeing the money come or seeing it go.
>
> "Changes are taking place and demanding such rapid adaptation of individuals that a new word has been coined to describe them — rapidation ... Are we ready for this state of electronic living? It's almost here."

An article from Hempstead, New York titled "Banking Without Cash a Reality":

> "The long-awaited 'cashless society' already has arrived here in Hempstead and five other communities on Long Island's North Shore. Most financial experts say that the idea of exchanging money electronically not only works but sooner or later will be commonplace across the country ... The entire process takes only about 20 seconds, and the only paper involved is the customer's receipt ... Spokesman William J.

Gibney notes that about half of his bank's 5,000 customers use their cards, called Instant Transaction, or IT, on a regular basis."

Another item from the Associated Press, dateline Denver, reads in part:

"Bankers who once talked of a cashless society now are moving toward what they hope will become a checkless one. The move toward an electronic system of buying and banking is already under way in scattered areas of the country, including Colorado, Louisiana, Hawaii and Ohio. Arizona is next on the list ... The National Science Foundation, in a study released in February said that eventually 70 percent of the current volume of 28 billion check payments will be handled by 'electronic substitutes.'"

A Motorola paper dated September 8, 1977 reads in part:

"Welcome To Government Electronics Division ... A series of numbers and letters (five 6-digit numbers) are used in transmitting and receiving messages via the Motorola Data Security Module ... Durrell W. Hillis, GED's Program Development Manager for Secure Communications emphasized, 'Electronic funds transfer applies not just on the bank-to-bank basis ... There is no turning back from an increasing

THE MARK AND THE NUMBER 135

> dependence on computer systems ... because of this new kind of data encryption which Motorola utilizes in its new hardware, it is possible to absolutely protect data while it is being transmitted from computer to computer, or terminal to terminal, anywhere in the world."

Before long, all credit cards will be replaced by an international computer card. This is already taking place in Europe. Quoting from the April 12, 1982 edition of *Newsweek:*

> "They are thicker and somewhat heavier than the ordinary credit card — but 'Smart Cards' are plastic money that can 'think' as well as 'talk.' Now being test-marketed in France, the Smart Card contains a micro-memory and a micro-computer in a silicon chip no bigger than a dime. Like the coded magnetic strip of a normal card, the microchip remembers its account number and credit limits. But the Smart Card can do much more; it can store encoded data on up to 180 separate accounts, and it can continuously compute debits, credits and current balances for each of them. Inserted in a retailer's electronic reader, the card functions as a credit card that is virtually invulnerable to fraud. Plugged into the customer's home computer and linked to his bank by phone, the card can transfer funds, pay bills and balance his checking account ... in the United States, CitiBank and Chase Manhattan are interested, and First Bank

> *Systems of Minneapolis, Minn., will begin its own experiment with telebanking this summer..."*

The preceding information reports of past years illustrate that our present course in world economics, politics and religion is being guided by a master plan. The first computer code mark on merchandise items appeared five years before computer checkout counters were installed. This was no coincidence. Expressions like EFTs and SDRs were in common usage ten years before they became standard banking operations.

Networks are being established to impose instant, worldwide business operations in all phases of the financial structure through Electronic Funds Transfers that utilize nothing more than marks and numbers.

The missing link in the prophetic chain tying the apocalyptic pattern of developments in the computer field to Revelation 13 is a universal computer mark and number. A nationally-known editorial writer, William Safire, reported on a federally sponsored identification program that appears similar to the beast system that is prophesied in Revelation. This editorial appeared on September 9, 1982 in *The New York Times:*

> *"In a well-meaning effort to curb the employment of illegal aliens, and with the hearty good wishes of editorialists who ordinarily pride themselves on guarding against the intrusion of government into the private lives of individual Americans, Congress is about to take this generation's*

longest step toward totalitarianism. The first step downward on the Simpson staircase to 'Big Brotherdom' is the requirement that within three years the federal government come up with a 'secure system to determine employment eligibility in the United States.' Despite denials, that means a national identity card. Nobody who is pushing the bill admits that — on the contrary, all sorts of 'safeguards' and rhetorical warnings about not having to carry an identity card on one's person at all times are festooned on the bill. Much is made of the use of passports, Social Security cards, and driver's licenses as 'preferred' forms of identification, but anyone who takes the trouble to read this legislation can see that the disclaimers are intended to help the medicine go down.

"Most American citizens are being led to believe that only aliens will be required to show 'papers.' But how can a prospective employer tell who is an alien? If the applicant could say, 'I'm an American, I don't have any card,' the new control system would immediately break down.

"The very basis of the proposed law is the notion that individuals must carry verifiable papers — most likely a card keyed to a 'new government data bank' — to prove eligibility for work ... Most Americans see no danger at all in a national-identity card.

"Most people even like the idea of a piece of plastic that tells the world, and themselves, who they are. 'I'm me,' says the little card. 'I'm entitled to all the benefits that

go with being provably and demonstrably me.

"Good citizens — the ones who vote regularly and who don't get into auto accidents — might get a gold card. Once the down staircase is set in place, the temptation to take each next step will be irresistible. Certainly every business would want to ask customers to insert their identity cards into the whizbang credit checker.

"Banks, phone companies, schools, and hotels would take advantage of the obvious utility of the document that could not be counterfeited. Law enforcement and tax collection would surely be easier because the federal government would know at all times exactly where everybody was and what they were spending ...

"We are entering the computer age. Combined with a national identity card — an abuse of power that Peter Rodino professes to oppose in the house, as he makes it inevitable — government computers and data banks pose a threat to personal liberty. Though aimed against 'undocumented workers,' the computer tattoo will be pressed on you and me."

We do believe that the day when everyone in the world will work, buy and sell using code marks and numbers is very near — perhaps no further than a few years at best. The most important thing for the individual, in view of all these things, is to be ready to go when Christ calls. The Bible declares in I Thessalonians 4:13-18, that if you will believe that

Jesus is the Christ, the Son of God, who died for sins and rose again from the grave, and then accept Him as Lord and Savior, you will be ready for whatever comes in your present life, or in the life to come.

12
A PRESIDENT FOR PLANET EARTH

In the last book of the Bible we are informed that four horsemen of the Apocalypse will come upon the world scene to present factors that will make a supreme president of planet Earth desirable. We refer first to Revelation 6:2:

"And I saw, and behold a white horse: and he that sat on him had a bow; and a crown was given unto him: and he went forth conquering, and to conquer.'

Revelation 19:11 informs us that God's Messiah, the Lord Jesus Christ, will return to this planet on a white horse, but the white horse rider of Revelation 6:2 is a false messiah. He is a savior that the nations select. This man's crown is given to him, and he will receive his high office by appointment from a council representing 10 powerful nations. The second rider brings news of famine and inflation, and it is with his appearance that a new world economic system goes into effect to save the nations from total chaos. It is seemingly no coincidence that the chief advocate of

A PRESIDENT FOR PLANET EARTH

a new world money system today is the Trilateral Commission, an alliance of 10 nations (Japan, the United States, Canada, and seven Common Market nations). We quote from the November 14, 1977 edition of *The Wall Street Transcript:*

> *"Bancor: Its Potential As An International Currency — A new low for the dollar, the political and social demand for reflation in the '80's, lower real world output in 1978, the transition of effective power from the International Monetary fund to the Bank for International Settlements, all add up to the potential introduction of the Bancor, a new international money form, between June and September of 1978. The major proponent of Bancor is the Trilateral Commission. They have described themselves as 'private citizens of Western Europe, North America and Japan, formed to foster closer cooperation among the three regions on common problems.' This group is an economic study group sponsored by establishment banking personalities. Seventeen members of this group, plus President Carter, make up our present administration. It was the Trilateral Commission who originally made the suggestion to the International Monetary fund to sell gold. Their recent proposal, therefore, must be given serious consideration as a blueprint of future events ... In order to prepare psychologically to accept Bancor, other monetary reserve items must appear less acceptable ...*

> *Should 1978 develop into a year of declining world economic statistics, then Bancor's time may have arrived ... The Bancor follows too closely on the heels of the SDR. A promise to pay, validated by restriction of supply only, like the German backing of a new currency after the great inflation, will have only a short-term effect. It will, however, magnify the next four-year cycle creating a greater demand after June of 1980 for refuge and alternative currency items."*

Four years from 1978 brings us again to 1982, evidently the target date, according to the preceding report, that the Trilateral Commission has set for the arrival of a new world money system under the code name Bancor. A communications system via satellite under the code name SWIFT has already been established to handle EFT, and as we have previously noted, it is rapidly being enlarged.

Even the secular press can no longer ignore the similarity in developing world conditions to Bible prophecy relating to the last days. *The Los Angeles Times Services* recently carried a story titled "Doomsday Fever Rising Among Millions," and we quote just a portion:

> *"The old bearded prophet of doom with his sandwich-board message declaring that the end is near has been around for a long time. But now, millions — many who would not classify themselves as religious — are taking the message seriously, or are at least fascinated by its possibilities. With the aid of*

the modern news media, a foreboding scenario spawned by Bible prophecy has been spread: events are coming together in the exact pattern that signals the end of this age and the return of Jesus Christ ... From Baptists and Pentecostalists to Seventh-Day Adventists ... there is widespread agreement that signs of the 'last days' are abundant. They cite instances of crime and immorality, famine and earthquakes, increased popularity of the occult and 'false religions.' In fact, hardly a crisis or world political development occurs without it being seen as one more sign of the end. Most important is the return of Jews to their homeland — the establishment of the state of Israel in 1948. Some groups have believed that the final Battle of Armageddon will come within a generation of that date. But the length of a generation, in Bible reckoning, is variously interpreted. Instead of 1948, some have placed emphasis on 1967 as the departure point (the beginning of the last generation), the year Israel took full control of Jerusalem. If Israel is 'God's timepiece,' as the Bible prophecy teachers and preachers say, there is usually caution taken nevertheless to avoid setting the alarm for a specific year."

But it is not only the Christians who are observing the signs of the times who are sounding the alarm. *The Smithsonian* magazine recently stated that there seems to be no possible way this civilization can last beyond the year 2000. As nuclear weapons become more widely disseminated, the only hope world leaders see for survival is a dictatorship in which every person in the world will be so closely supervised by a world government there can be no chance of a world atomic war. We brought out in a previous chapter how this would be possible, and consider the following news release by UPI, dateline Cambridge, Mass., November 3, 1975:

> "A nuclear arms expert says a very nasty kind of world government may be the only way to keep the world from blowing itself up in a nuclear war. Writing in the November issue of Harvard Magazine, five panelists from Harvard University and the Massachusetts Institute of Technology said they believed nuclear war in some form will erupt before 1999. 'A very nasty kind of world government may be necessary if we are to survive in the world I see ahead,' wrote one of the participants, George Rathjens, an MIT professor. 'It would take an enormous surrender of sovereignty to bring nuclear proliferation under control ... a radical change in our whole lifestyle, meaning the surrender of most democratic values and the addition of rather brutal methods to keep the nuclear threat under control. Such a harsh government is a very grim prospect ... ' said Rathjens, the former chief scientist and deputy director for the Advanced Research Project Agency for the Department of Defense."

A PRESIDENT FOR PLANET EARTH

To demonstrate how the media is reporting unmistak-able signs of catastrophe and events leading up to Arma-geddon, we refer to end-of-the-year articles in just one newspaper, *The Daily Oklahoman,* December 26, 1985:

1. Natural Disasters Hit Populated Spots in 1985: Nature raged with unusual ferocity in 1985, killing more than 40,000 people in three outbursts. Yet slow death from famine remained a greater threat, claiming hundreds of thousands in Africa despite an outpouring of international aid and a return of rain. It was the most disastrous year since 1976, when major earthquakes struck Guatemala, China, and Italy."

2. 1985's Storms Were Costly: Five hurricanes staggered the United States with billions of dollars in damage in 1985, while mudslides, floods and tornadoes claimed heavy loss of life. Puerto Rico may have suffered the year's heaviest human toll when rain-induced mudslides engulfed the shantytown of Mamayes and other south-coast communities October 6-7. The death toll in Puerto Rico stands at 186, the Federal Emergency Management Agency said, with hundreds still reported missing. An exact total may never be known. Property damage has been estimated at nearly $500 million in the deluge.

Actually there were seven hurricanes that struck the Eastern seaboard of the United States in 1985.

3. Terrorism: 1985 the Worst Year Yet for Fatalities: *Terrorists killed more than 600 people in 1985 hijackings, bombings, assassinations and sabotage. Even the Soviet Union became a target. Brian Jenkins, a terrorism expert, said it was "the worst year yet. The first nine months of 1985 will certainly equal or surpass 1984 in the volume of terrorist acts, and will equal or surpass 1983 in terms of the number of fatalities — and 1983 was the bloodiest year on record. This has been a very rough year in terms of casualties." According to U.S. congressional figures, terrorist acts were carried out against 77 countries in 1985; as of October, more than 600 people had died worldwide. "There is today no people, no government, no diplomat, no traveler who can count himself immune from the terrorists," said U.S. ambassador to the United Nations, Vernon Walter.*

The computer is more and more controlling the activities of man, both on this earth and in the heavens.

Coming into being is a computer-television system that will watch people in their own homes, even after the television set is turned off. We refer to the October edition of *D,* a magazine of over 200 pages published in Dallas, Texas. The article by Rowland Stiteler was headlined: "Look at what is coming into your living room. When cable comes to Dallas next year, it will carry first-run movies, 24-hour news and sports — maybe even you":

A PRESIDENT FOR PLANET EARTH

One fifty-six a.m. It is quiet in the command post. Two members of the security force sit motionless, staring into a bank of a dozen television screens. They have been trained to be alert for anomalies in the community; anything which threatens security will be sensed electronically in seconds. The computer tells them that most of the residents are asleep. The guards can see which doors are open — or closed. The computer can tell them instantly if a fire is developing in any of the domiciles. It tells them if someone needs medical help, and when someone has set his thermostat too high or too low. It has the capability to monitor, and even control, electrical consumption in every sector. The community functions like one giant living organism:

The computer is its brain, and miles of cable, wired into every building, its central nervous system. There is very little in the community to which the command post sentinels don't have access. Walls have given way to wires. Privacy has given way to security. The computer controls everything. This is the embodiment of an Orwellian dream.

The computer is also making its presence known in outer space. New computer technology and laser breakthroughs have influenced our government to make plans for war in the heavens. An item in the April 1984 bulletin of The Research Institute of America is headlined: "A Year Closer To Star Wars Defense — Pentagon and high tech planners have pushed ahead with President Reagan's controversial 'Star Wars' missile defense system."

The super Fifth Generation computer proposed in the book, *The Enchanted Loom*, could be considered to be science fiction if it were not for the fact that its author, Dr. Robert Jastrow, is one of the leading scientists of our time. He is the founder of NASA's Goddard Institute for Space Studies, professor of astronomy at Columbia University, and Earth Sciences at Dartmouth College. We begin quoting from page 159 of his book:

> *"In theory, computers could have been built long ago with gates having many inputs, just like the human brain. However, even a small computer of this kind would need hundreds of billions of separate wires for its gate-to-gate connections.*
>
> *"A computer with billions of wires would be impossible to build in practice. The new chips change all that. In these chips there are no wires; the connections are microscopically small. This development ... is a breakthrough in computer evolution, because it makes it possible to build a computer with gates that work like the gates in the human brain. Such computers will come into existence in the 1990s ...*
>
> *"They will match the human mind in many respects, and will possess attributes of intelligent life — responsiveness to the world around them, the ability to learn by experience, and quick grasp of new ideas.*
>
> *"Will they be living organisms? Most people would say that a computer can never*

be a living organism, because it has no feelings or emotions; it does not eat, or move, or grow ...

"Most of these attributes could easily be built into computers if they were desired ... if its batteries run low, it can be programmed to move over to an electrical outlet and plug itself in for a snack ... Feelings and emotions also can be built into the computer ...

"I believe that in a larger cosmic perspective, going beyond the earth and its biological creatures, the true attributes of intelligent life will be seen to be those that are shared by man and the computer — a response to stimuli, absorption of information around the world, and flexible behavior under changing conditions.

"The brain that possesses these attributes may be made of water and carbon-chain molecules, and housed in fragile shell of bone, as our brain is; or it may be made of metallic silicon, and housed in plastic; but if it reacts to the world around it, and grows through experience, it is alive.

"The era of carbon-chemistry life is drawing to a close on the earth and a new era of silicon-based life — indestructible, immortal, infinitely expandable — is beginning. By the turn of the century, ultra-intelligent machines will be working in partnership with our best minds on all the serious problems of the day, in an unbeatable combination of brute reasoning power and human intuition ...

> *"One sees a vision of mammoth brains that have soaked up the wisdom of the human race and gone on from there ... Perhaps man can join forces with the computers to create a brain that combines the accumulated wisdom of the human mind with the power of the machine ...*
>
> *"This hybrid intelligence would be the progenitor of a new race ... a bold scientist will be able to tap the contents of his mind and transfer them into the lattices of a computer. Because mind is the essence of being, it can be said that this scientist has entered the computer, and that he now dwells in it.*
>
> *"At last the human brain, ensconced in a computer, has been liberated from the weaknesses of the mortal flesh ... Man need not wait a thousand years to reach the stars; the stars will come to him."*

Of the beast that will take control of the earth before Christ returns, we read:

> *"And he had power to give life unto the image of the beast, that the image of the beast should both speak, and cause that as many as would not worship the image of the beast should be killed. And he causeth all, both small and great, rich and poor, free and bond, to receive a mark in their right hand, or in their foreheads. And that no man might buy or sell, save he that had the mark, or the name of the beast, or the number of his name"* (Rev. 13:15-17).

A PRESIDENT FOR PLANET EARTH

Will the Antichrist attempt to create a new generation of immortal computerized human beings? It appears that biblical prophecy in this regard is very similar to that envisioned by Dr. Jastrow and others.

In any event, scientists are now working feverishly to fulfill man's demand for bigger, better and more intelligent computers and God has said, what man has imagined, that he can do.

The Doomsday message is coming mostly from the news media. The only hope they see in averting catastrophe is a world dictator, a president of planet Earth, who will institute a very nasty kind of world government. It is no wonder that this worldly dictator is identified in Scripture as "the Beast."

His government will be nasty indeed, because it will be demanded of every individual that he worship him as a god or be killed, and everyone will be commanded to be branded with a mark or a number. This, we are being told even today, is the only alternative to nuclear destruction.

But, there is another alternative. This alternative is neither a doomsday nor a beast-like world dictator. It is a message of hope and good will from God to all men ... John 3:16:

> *"For God so loved the world, that he gave His only begotten Son, that whosoever believeth on him, should not perish, but have eternal life."*

About the Authors

Dr. David Webber is the Pastor-Director-President of the Southwest Radio Church of the Air in Oklahoma City, Oklahoma.

He received his degree in theology from Oklahoma City University and is the author of more than 40 books and pamphlets.

Through the years he has been in demand as a public speaker in churches and Bible conferences.

Southwest Radio Church was founded in April, 1933, by Dr. E.F. Webber, the late father of David Webber.

He was born on February 17, 1931. He grew up in a Christian home as his father was a pastor, evangelist and founder of The Southwest Radio Church of the Air.

He was pastor of Calvary Tabernacle in Oklahoma City form 1964 to 1973 but gave up his pastorate to devote full time to the radio ministry.

The Southwest Radio Church produces a 30-minute, five-day-a-week program that is heard over a network of more than 130 stations, reaching from coast to coast. It is one of the oldest Christian broadcasts of its kind. David Webber assumed full-

ABOUT THE AUTHORS

time duties in the ministry of broadcasting after the home-going of his father in 1959.

Rev. Noah Hutchings for the past 35 years has been active in research and writing for daily radio programs for Southwest Radio Church, where he also serves as office manager.

He speaks on specific topics in the light of biblical truth and on prophetic subjects in various meetings throughout the nation.

Rev. Hutchings is editor of *The Gospel Truth*, a monthly publication of the radio ministry. The publication is read and reproduced in the United States and several foreign countries. It is translated for the Spanish-speaking people as *Profecias Biblicas*.

Rev. Hutchings also leads Bible-study tours to Israel and other lands and is recognized for his great knowledge of the Middle East.

More Faith-Building Books *from* Huntington House

America Betrayed! by Marlin Maddoux. This hard-hitting book exposes the forces in our country which seek to destroy the family, the schools and our values. This book details exactly how the news media manipulates your mind. Marlin Maddoux is the host of the popular, national radio talk show "Point of View."

A Reasonable Reason to Wait, by Jacob Aranza, is a frank, definitive discussion on premarital sex — from the biblical viewpoint. God speaks specifically about premarital sex, according to the author. The Bible also provides a healing message for those who have already been sexually involved before marriage. This book is a must reading for every young person — and also for parents — who really want to known the biblical truth on this important subject.

Backward Masking Unmasked, by Jacob Aranza. Rock'n'Roll music affects tens of millions of young people and adults in America and around the world. This music is laced with lyrics exalting drugs, the occult, immorality, homosexuality, violence and rebellion. But there is more sinister danger in this music according to the author. It's called "backward masking." Numerous rock groups employ this mind-influencing technique in their recordings. Teenagers by the millions — who spend hours each day listening to rock music — aren't even aware the messages are there. The author clearly exposes these dangers.

Backward Masking Unmasked, (cassette tape) by Jacob Aranza. Hear actual satanic messages and judge for yourself.

Beast, by Dan Betzer. This is the story of the rise to power of the future world dictator — the antichrist. This novel plots a dark web of intrigue which begins with the suicide-death of Adolf Hitler who believed he had been chosen to be the world dictator. Yet, in his last days, he spoke of "the man who will come after me." Several decades later that man, Jacque Catroux, head of the European economic system, appears on the world scene. He had been born the day Hitler died, conceived by the seed of Lucifer himself. In articulate prose, the author describes the "disappearance" of the Christians from the earth; the horror and hopelessness which followed that event; and the bitter agony of life on earth after all moral and spiritual restraints are removed.

Devil Take the Youngest by Winkie Pratney. This book reveals the war on children that is being waged in America and the world today. Pratney, a world-renowned author, teacher and conference speaker, says there is a spirit of Moloch loose in the land. The author relates distinct parallels of the ancient worship of Moloch — where little children were sacrificed screaming into his burning fire — to the tragic killing and kidnapping of children today. This timely book says the war on children has its roots in the occult.

Globalism: America's Demise, by William Bowen, Jr. The Globalists — some of the most powerful people on earth — have plans to totally eliminate God, the family, and the United States as we know it today. Globalism is the vehicle the humanists are using to implement their secular humanistic philosophy to bring about their one-world government. The four goals of Globalism are: 1) a one-world government; 2) a new world religion; 3) a new economic system; 4) a new race of people for the new world order. This book alerts Christians to what Globalists have planned for them.

God's Timetable for the 1980's, by Dr. David Webber. This book presents the end-time scenario as revealed in God's Word. It deals with a wide spectrum of subjects including the dangers of the New Age Movement, end-time weather changes, outer space, robots and biocomputers in prophecy. According to the author, the mysterious number 666 is occurring more and more frequently in world communications, banking and business. This number will one day polarize the computer code marks and identification numbering systems of the Antichrist, he says.

Hearts on Fire, by Jimmy Phillips. What is God doing throughout the world? Where is revival taking place? What is the heart's cry of the people? Phillips answers these and other important questions in this delightful book. During his travels as a missionary-evangelist, he has ministered both in the rag cities of India and the largest church in the world, which is in Korea. As you read his story, your heart will be set on fire as you take a fresh look at the world through his eyes.

How to Cope When You Can't by Don Gossett is a guide to dealing with the everyday stresses and pressures of life. Gossett, a well-known Christian author and evangelist, draws from many personal experiences in this book which brings hope and encouragement for victory in our Lord. The author deals with such contemporary subjects as coping with guilt, raising children, financial difficulties, poverty, a sectarian spirit, the devil's devices, pride, fear and inadequacy, sickness, sorrow, enemies and other real problems. This book is a must for those Christians who want to be victorious.

More Rock, Country & Backward Masking Unmasked by Jacob Aranza. Aranza's first book, *Backward Masking Unmasked* was a national bestseller. It clearly exposed the backward satanic messages included in a lot of rock and roll music. Now, in the sequel, Aranza gives a great deal of new information on backward messages. Also, for the first time in Christian literature, he takes a hard look at the content, meaning and dangers of country music. "Rock, though filled with satanism, sex and drugs ... has a hard time keeping up with the cheatin', drinkin' and one-night stands that continue to dominate country music," the author says.

Murdered Heiress ... Living Witness, by Dr. Petti Wagner. The victim of a sinister kidnapping and murder plot, the Lord miraculously gave her life back to her. Dr. Wagner — heiress to a large fortune — was kidnapped, tortured, beaten, electrocuted and died. A doctor signed her death certificate, yet she lives today!

Natalie — The Miracle Child by Barry and Cathy Beaver. This is the heartwarming, inspirational story of little Natalie Beaver — God's miracle child — who was born with virtually no chance to live — until God intervened! When she was born, her internal organs were outside her body. The doctors said she would never survive. Yet, God performed a miracle and Natalie is healed today. Now, as a pre-teen, she is a gifted singer and sings the praises of a miracle-working God.

Rest From the Quest, by Elissa Lindsey McClain. This is the candid account of a former New Ager who spent the first 29 years of her life in the New Age Movement, the occult and Eastern mysticism. This is an incredible inside look at what really goes on in the New Age Movement.

Take Him to the Streets, by Jonathan Gainsbrugh. Well-known author David Wilkerson says this book is "... immensely helpful ..." and "... should be read ..." by all Christians who yearn to win lost people to Christ, particularly through street ministry. Effective ministry techniques are detailed in this how-to book on street preaching. Carefully read and applied, this book will help you reach others.

The Agony of Deception, by Ron Rigsbee. This is the story of a young man who became a woman through surgery and now, through the grace of God, is a man again. Share this heartwarming story of a young man as he struggles through the deception of an altered lifestyle only to find hope and deliverance in the grace of God.

The Divine Connection, by Dr. Donald Whitaker. This is a Christian guide of life extension. It specifies biblical principles on how to feel better and live longer and shows you how to experience Divine health, a happier life, relief from stress, a better appearance, a healthier outlook on life, a zest for living and a sound emotional life.

The Hidden Dangers of the Rainbow, by Constance Cumbey. A national #1 bestseller, this is a vivid exposé of the New Age Movement which is dedicated to wiping out Christianity and establishing a one-world order. This movement — a vast network of tens of thousands of occultic and other organizations — meets the test of prophecy concerning the Antichrist.

The Hidden Dangers of the Rainbow Tape, by Constance Cumbey. Mrs. Cumbey, a trial lawyer from Detroit, Michigan, gives inside information on the New Age Movement in this teaching tape.

The Miracle of Touching, by Dr. John Hornbrook. Most everyone enjoys the special attention that a loving touch brings. Throughout this encouraging book the author explains what touching others through love — under the careful guidance of the Lord Jesus Christ — can accomplish. Dr. Hornbrook urges Christians to reach out and touch someone — family members, friends, prisoners — and do it to the glory of God, physically, emotionally and spiritually.

The Twisted Cross, by Joseph Carr. One of the most important works of our decade, The Twisted Cross clearly documents the occult and demonic influence on Adolf Hitler and the Third Reich which led to the killing of more than 6 million Jews. The author even gives specifics of the bizarre way in which Hitler actually became demon-possessed.

Who Will Rise Up? by Jed Smock. This is the incredible — and sometimes hilarious — story of Jed Smock, who with his wife, Cindy, has preached the uncompromising gospel on the malls and lawns of hundreds of university campuses throughout this land. They have been mocked, rocked, stoned, mobbed, beaten, jailed, cursed and ridiculed by the students. Yet this former university professor and his wife have seen the miracle-working power of God transform thousands of lives on university campuses.

Yes, send me the following books:

___ copy (copies) of America Betrayed! @ $5.95 =$_____
___ copy (copies) of A Reasonable Reason To Wait @ $4.95 =$_____
___ copy (copies) of Backward Masking Unmasked @ $5.95 =$_____
___ copy (copies) of Backward Masking Unmasked Cassette Tape @ $6.95 =$_____
___ copy (copies) of Beast @ $6.95 =$_____
___ copy (copies) of Computers and the Beast of Revelation @ $6.95 =$_____
___ copy (copies) of Devil Take the Youngest @ $6.95 =$_____
___ copy (copies) of Edmund Burke and the Natural Law @ $7.95 =$_____
___ copy (copies) of Globalism: America's Demise @ $6.95 =$_____
___ copy (copies) of God's Timetable for the 1980's @ $5.95 =$_____
___ copy (copies) of Hearts on Fire @ $5.95 =$_____
___ copy (copies) of Honor Thy Father? @ $6.95 =$_____
___ copy (copies) of How to Cope When You Can't @ $6.95 =$_____
___ copy (copies) of How to Grow Up Spiritually @ $6.95 =$_____
___ copy (copies) of More Rock, Country & Backward Masking @ $5.95 =$_____
___ copy (copies) of More Rock, Country & Backward Masking Tape @ $6.95 =$_____
___ copy (copies) of Murdered Heiress ... Living Witness @ $6.95 =$_____
___ copy (copies) of Natalie @ $4.95 =$_____
___ copy (copies) of Need a Miracle? @ $5.95 =$_____
___ copy (copies) of Rest From the Quest @ $5.95 =$_____
___ copy (copies) of Take Him to the Streets @ $6.95 =$_____
___ copy (copies) of The Agony of Deception @ $6.95 =$_____
___ copy (copies) of The Divine Connection @ $4.95 =$_____
___ copy (copies) of The Great Falling Away Today @ $6.95 =$_____
___ copy (copies) of The Hidden Dangers of the Rainbow @ $6.95 =$_____
___ copy (copies) of The Hidden Dangers of the Rainbow Seminar Tapes @ $19.95 =$_____
___ copy (copies) of The Miracle of Touching @ $5.95 =$_____
___ copy (copies) of The Twisted Cross @ $7.95 =$_____
___ copy (copies) of Where Were You When I Was Hurting? @ $6.95 =$_____
___ copy (copies) of Who Will Rise Up? @ $5.95 =$_____

AT BOOKSTORES EVERYWHERE or order directly from Huntington House, Inc., P.O. Box 53788, Lafayette, LA 70505

Send check/money order or for faster service VISA/Mastercard orders call toll-free 1-800-572-8213. Add: Freight and handling, $1.00 for the first book ordered, 50¢ for each additional book.

Name _____ Enclosed is $_____ including postage.
Address _____
City _____ State and ZIP _____